VISIONS OF HOPE

Apocalyptic Themes
from Biblical Times

DONALD SNEEN

AUGSBURG PUBLISHING HOUSE
MINNEAPOLIS, MINNESOTA

VISIONS OF HOPE

Copyright © 1978 Augsburg Publishing House

Library of Congress Catalog Card No. 77-84098

International Standard Book No. 0-8066-1624-5

Scripture quotations unless otherwise noted are from the Revised Standard Version of the Bible, copyright 1946, 1952, and 1971 by the Division of Christian Education of the National Council of Churches.

MANUFACTURED IN THE UNITED STATES OF AMERICA

Contents

Preface

In 1890 a preacher named Wovoka appeared among the Sioux Indians in western South Dakota. They greeted him as the son of the Great Spirit, the Messiah who had returned to life after his death at the hands of the white men years before. Wovoka told his disheartened people, who had lost their buffalo and the best of their land, that a new world was coming the following spring. It would come like a cloud in a whirlwind and crush out the present evil world dominated by the whites. In the new world all the dead Indians would come back to life, the bison would return, and the Sioux nation would prosper. The Sioux, who previously had lost all hope, began to prepare for this new world. They held ghost dances in which the dancers claimed that they saw their dead relatives and talked to them.

The Sioux Indian experience, described so vividly in *Black Elk Speaks,* is a modern example of an apocalyptic movement in American culture. The words of the visionary spoken to a people in a hopeless situation inspired the Sioux to plan for a future and a hope. Hope in the future is necessary for human survival, whether individual or group. Where there is no vision the people perish! The vision of the apocalyptic seer releases a dynamic which again and again in history has renewed hope among the hopeless.

This experience was particularly true among the Hebrews and early Christians. A whole body of literature, some twenty to thirty writings, was written from this experience. Apocalyptic literature originated with the ancient Hebrews, coming into full bloom in the distressing centuries just before the Christian era. The early Christians, who also lived through persecutions, inherited Hebrew traditions and hopes. Thus, early Christian literature, most notably in the New Testament, shows a strong apocalyptic flavor. The outstanding example is the book of Revelation, whose Greek title is "The Apocalypse."

Unfortunately, the prevailing view toward this apocalyptic literature in general, and the book of Revelation in particular, has been one of ignorance. Most denominations ignore this literature, leaving it to sensationalists to expound. This volume is written to assist readers who are seeking to understand more fully the issues, events, and literature of the exciting and complex period that is also the dawn of the Christian era.

For a variety of reasons, apocalyptic attitudes and ideas are widespread in our generation. Bumper stickers, with flashy apocalyptic messages about the rapture, appear on automobiles. Books dealing with apocalyptic themes as direct prophecies are widely read. Preachers who interpret Daniel and Revelation as though their writers were predictive sharpshooters for twentieth century events often draw large audiences. This thoroughly futurist interpretation is not biblical enough. It all too easily ignores the sweat, blood, and tears of the early martyrs and fellow sufferers among God's people at the dawn of the Christian era. In addition, it is geared more to human curiosity than to Christian faith, and it appeals more to fear than to hope. Christian life is not renewed by fear and despair, but only in the hope that is enduring and sure. Believers are called to live on the summit, inspired by a vision of hope, in order to avoid the abyss. In a modern age when the foundations are shaking and many believe the world has a terminal illness, the biblical apocalyptic writers call us not to despair, but to trust in the "God of hope."

Donald Sneen

1 What Is Apocalyptic?

Many shall run to and fro, and knowledge shall increase.
DANIEL 12:4.

These words were written more than two thousand years ago. They had profound meaning for Daniel, the apocalyptist who wrote them. They also have a profound meaning for us in our modern world. For the statement of the ancient writer is being fulfilled in an amazing way in our very own lifetime.

Reflecting on the "many," let's examine population growth. There were probably between 200 and 250 million human inhabitants on earth at the beginning of the Christian era. This figure did not double until about A.D. 1600. By 1820 the world population finally reached one billion. It reached two billion in 1930, three billion in 1960, four billion in 1976, and projections estimate that it will continue to climb so that the world population will be between six and seven billion by the year 2000. While the population soars, the world's capacity to feed its increasing billions, even with modern technology and scientific agricultural methods, cannot keep pace. Terms like "population bomb" and "demographic doom" are commonly used to describe the population explosion. The third and fourth horsemen of the Apocalypse, representing famine and death, loom larger and larger on the horizon with each passing year (Rev. 6:5-8).

The apocalyptist stated that "many shall run to and fro." In 6000 B.C. the fastest transportation available to man over long distances was the camel caravan, which averaged about eight miles per hour. About 1600 B.C., when the chariot was invented, the maximum speed reached about twenty miles per hour. This record held for thousands of years. Even the first steam locomotive, which came on the scene in 1825, could only do thirteen miles per hour. It wasn't until the 1880s that man, with the help of a more advanced steam locomotive, managed to reach speeds of one hundred miles per hour. Within fifty years that rate had quadrupled, with aviators flying at four hundred miles per hour by 1938. In a mere twenty years, it doubled again, with man flying faster than sound and sonic booms becoming common annoyances. By the 1960s, men in space capsules were circling the earth and later the moon at 18,000 miles per hour. When this rate of progress is plotted on a graph, the line representing speed increase in this generation leaps off the page.

"And knowledge shall increase." We moderns express this reality by the term "knowledge explosion." If we define knowledge as "the aggregate of known facts, data, and principles," the increase has been astounding. Human knowledge doubled between 1600 and 1900, doubled again between 1900 and 1950, and by 1960 had doubled again. Estimates and projections are always risky, but certain estimates are that knowledge will multiply thirty-two times over between 1950 and the year 2000.

The rapid advances in science and the great growling engines of technology are the causes of the amazing changes that now threaten to engulf us like a fire storm. Transcience, rather than permanence or even gradual change, now becomes the norm. The carousel of change produces not only a turnover in automobile models and techniques in medicine, but also in people's world views and life-styles. Older people, who in more stable societies acted as the bearers of tradition, end up on the sidelines today, simply being "out of it." The experiments and life-style of the young get much more attention than the attitudes and habits of the aged. The child's character is molded less and less by the parents and more and more by the modern media and exposure to outside influences.

People vary in their response to these changes and the accelerating pace of life. Most welcome the labor and time-saving gadgets and devices; some search for immortality in a man-made world through transplant surgery. Others can't adjust to the dizzy pace, and begin to do strange irrational things. There are rich people who playact poverty, computer programmers who turn on with LSD, and professing witches who nevertheless turn on light switches! The technology which gives man more and more control over nature shows him to be less and less the master of himself. Voices of warning, some irrational, but others that speak very knowledgeably, remind us about the approaching end. Paul Ehrlich warns of the death of the oceans, with mankind's end soon following. A whole generation has been born and grown to maturity since the atomic bombs were dropped on Hiroshima and Nagasaki. How will the end come, with a whimper or a bang?

These are the signs of an apocalyptic age. An apocalyptic time is an age when one world is dying, and another struggling to be born. A modern prophet like Herman Hesse observed this occurring as early as 1927 when he wrote in *Steppenwolf;*

Every age, every culture, every custom and tradition has its own character, its own weakness and its own strength, its beauties and ugliness; accepts certain sufferings as matters of course, puts up patiently with certain evil. Human life is reduced to real suffering, to hell, only when two ages, two cultures and religions overlap ... Now there are times when a whole generation is caught in this way between two ages, two modes of life, with the consequence that it loses all power to understand itself and has no standard, no security, no innocence.[1]

About A.D. 55 the apostle Paul wrote these words to the church at Corinth:

I mean, brethren, the appointed time has grown very short; from now on, let those who have wives live as though they had none, and those who mourn as though they were not mourning, and those who rejoice as though they were not rejoicing, and those who buy as though they had no goods, and those who deal with the world as though they had no dealings with it. For the form of this world is passing away (1 Cor. 7:29-31).

The common denominator for many people in the first century and our twentieth century is this apocalyptic attitude of mind that sees the end of our world as near. The world has a terminal illness, and cannot continue long on its present course. This means different things to different people, however. For the modern counterculture movement, it means an end to a technocracy that would encase us in a plastic and concrete world and program our behavior, and a vision of a new heaven and new earth that will open up the human imagination and experience to the wonder and glory of the natural and human world around us.[2] For others it means reading the Bible, especially the books of Daniel and Revelation, to find answers to questions about when and how the end of the world will come.[3] What should we do—open our eyes or open our Bibles?

The fact is that neither of these approaches is on target as far as biblical apocalyptic is concerned, though the second one claims to be. The counterculture's vision is of a new *human* consciousness that recaptures and affirms the wonder and excitement of the natural and human world. This is a reaction against the technocrats who measure progress only by human skyscrapers and supersonic planes at the expense of trees and flowers and birds and human sanity. There is much to applaud in their protest, but it is not a biblical view of the end. The second approach uses the Bible, or rather misuses it! The writers of Daniel and Revelation had a message about the end, but they were not predictive sharpshooters who were foretelling exact happenings two thousand years in the future. They had a powerful message for their time, and also for ours, provided we read and understand them from the standpoint of informed faith, and not ignorant curiosity. They should be read first of all from the context of their own time. After that, we are in a position to seek and apply their meaning for our time. A careful student of these two books, or any of the biblical books, asks two questions of the text. He asks first the historical question, "What did it mean when the book was written?" Then he asks the contemporary question, "What does it mean today?"

The fact is that there is a whole group of Jewish writings that may appropriately be called apocalyptic literature, and which deal with themes concerning the course of history and the end of the age. These Jewish books were written during the last two

centuries B.C. and the first century A.D. D. S. Russell lists sixteen
Jewish apocalyptic books from this period in addition to Daniel:

> 1 Enoch 1-36, 37-71, 72-82, 83-90, 91-108
> The Book of Jubilees
> The Sibylline Oracles, Book III
> The Testaments of the Twelve Patriarchs
> The Psalms of Solomon
> The Assumption of Moses
> The Martyrdom of Isaiah
> The Life of Adam and Eve, or The Apocalypse of Moses
> The Apocalypse of Abraham
> The Testament of Abraham
> 2 Enoch, or The Book of the Secrets of Enoch
> The Sibylline Oracles, Book IV
> 2 Esdras (also known as 4 Ezra)
> 2 Baruch, or the Apocalypse of Baruch
> 3 Baruch
> The Sibylline Oracles, Book V.[4]

There are also writings from the Jewish community at Qumran,
near the Dead Sea, that are apocalyptic in character. The most
outstanding example is the War Scroll, although several other
writings from that strange and interesting community have
apocalyptic features in varying degrees.

Other scholars have other lists. Exact agreement on which
books to include is almost impossible because the literature itself
is not that uniform in its style and content. There is a certain
fluid character about many of these writings. Therefore, one
should not be dogmatic about an exact list of apocalyptic books,
although certain ones like Daniel, Revelation, 1 Enoch, and
2 Esdras, to name a few of the more important ones, belong
unmistakably to this class of literature. However, there are cer-

tain characteristics of this literature that especially distinguish it. A discussion of these characteristics will be helpful in giving an informed answer to the question, What is apocalyptic?

Apocalyptic literature is always visionary in its origin and character. The visions reveal something about human destiny that has been a secret or a mystery; it has been guarded in heaven but will soon come to pass on earth. The vision experience consists of both "seeing" and "hearing" the vision that is interpreted by a heavenly angel. Thus vision and audition are joined in a dialog that may include several chapters in a book. The book of Revelation has a series of these great visions, beginning with the one where the writer is transported into the heavens and sees an open door (Rev. 4:1f.). The experience often produces a spiritual turmoil in the seer, who is filled with fear and dread over what is about to happen. Sometimes he even goes into a trance (Dan. 10). His excitement is reflected in what he writes and how he writes. Something momentous is about to take place. It will be earth-shaking in character, cosmic in its extent, and a mind-blowing reversal of all existing conditions. There is an urgency, even a crisis, because the time is short and the end appointed by God is near.

Because apocalyptic is communicating a heavenly message, its language is highly symbolic. Numbers have a very important function. Four represents the earth; six, one less than seven, is a human number; seven is a divine number; twelve represents Israel; forty is the length of one generation; seventy is the normal human life span. Sacred numbers and round figures are used elsewhere in the Bible, but even more frequently and mysteriously in apocalyptic. Gematria, a practice that assigns numerical value to the letters of a word, is occasionally found; Revelation 13:18 is an interesting example of this. Allegory is very common, and is developed in an imaginative and dramatic way. Nations

and individuals are represented as animals, while heavenly beings
or angels are represented as men. The prophets occasionally used
allegory. But the apocalyptic writer has built up the figures and
their interaction so that the drama is incomprehensible without
an interpreter.

Jewish apocalyptic writings are pseudonymous; that is, their
authors do not use their own names but take a name of a man
of God from the past and write under his assumed name. The
book of Joel, which has some apocalyptic features, is probably
the last Jewish work that was not pseudonymous. Various explanations for this pseudonymous character have been given.
R. H. Charles, a noted British scholar who studied apocalyptic
for forty years, suggests that it was due to the absolute supremacy
that the Law came to occupy in late Judaism. Prophecy had
ceased, and the voice of the prophet was no longer heard in
Israel (see 1 Macc. 4:46, 9:27, and 14:41). The prophets had made
their contribution, now the Law had assumed that function. God
had spoken his final word through the Law. This was the viewpoint of the religious leaders, the rabbis. Thus no new ideas were
acceptable, no matter how orthodox they were, unless they had
the imprimatur of the Law. Consequently, the apocalyptic visionaries issued their writings under the great names of the past, like
Enoch, Moses, Baruch, Daniel, and Ezra. This may seem like
plagiarism to moderns, but the literary ethics of the ancient world
were very different from those of the modern world. The Christian apocalypse is an exception to this practice. It is interesting
that the writer identifies himself in Revelation 1:9: "I John . . .
was on the island called Patmos on account of the word of God
and the testimony of Jesus."

Apocalyptic writers dealt with history in terms of world
epochs. The prophets preached to the nation of Israel; their
horizon of history generally ran back to the origin of national

Israel and forward to the day of the Lord when Israel would be first among the nations. But the apocalyptists pushed the horizons out both ways, back to creation and forward to the new heaven and new earth. They were cosmic rather than national in their horizons. Daniel 2 and 7 are examples of world history summarized in four epochs. In Daniel 2 the earthly kingdoms are portrayed as metals—gold, bronze, iron, and iron mixed with clay—which finally will be replaced with an eternal kingdom that shall not be destroyed; in Daniel 7 the same kingdoms are active animals, with the fourth one the most atrocious of all. 1 Enoch 85-90 is a summary of history, with particular emphasis on Israel, from the time of Adam to the Messiah. The main part of 2 Esdras (4 Ezra) consists of a series of seven visions in which the seer is instructed by the angel Uriel concerning the mysteries of the moral world and the end of this age. After the seventh vision, Ezra is told these words: "For the age has lost its youth, and the times begin to grow old. For the age is divided into twelve parts, and nine of its parts have already passed, as well as half of the tenth part; so two of its parts remain, besides half of the tenth part" (2 Esdras 14:10-12).

These visions of world history are not only dramatic but also dualistic. History is seen as an alternating succession of six black and six white waters in the vision of the cloud in 2 Baruch 53; the angel Ramiel explains to Baruch that these waters symbolize alternating bad and good periods of history, starting with Adam's fall and ending with the kingdom of God. The apocalyptists typically saw things and events in black and white, not in murky grays. They were dualistic in their vision and outlook. The universe is the place where the evil and good forces struggle for mastery and control. Satan—who is variously called the devil, Behemoth, Belial, and Leviathan—and his forces struggle against the Lord and his heavenly forces. Events in nature and history reflect this fierce, cosmic struggle which will eventually be won by the forces of the Lord and his heavenly host. Believers stand between the present evil age, which will pass away, and the age to come, which is God's eternal kingdom.

Finally the apocalyptists, in contrast with the prophets, were literary men. The prophets were told to go out and preach after they received their visions; their visions were calls to a public preaching ministry in Israel. But the apocalyptic seers were told to write down the vision, and to seal up the book until the end time (Dan. 12:4, and 2 Esdras 12:37f., 14:22 are a few examples). John was told to write his visions in a book and send it to the seven churches (Rev. 1:11); however, in the epilog we read these interesting words of instruction, "Do not seal up the words of the prophecy of this book, for the time is near" (Rev. 22:10).

Apocalyptic then is both an attitude of mind and a body of literature. As literature, it is visionary and highly symbolic in character, usually pseudonymous, and aims to interpret the course of history and reveal the end of the world-age. The events in Israel's history that shaped the mental attitude and eventually produced this literature are discussed in the next chapter.

2 The Context of Hebrew Apocalyptic

The Bible is a written record of God's revelation of himself to a people in history. For Orthodox Jews, life started with Abraham, their traditional ancestor, to whom God revealed himself (Gen. 12:1ff.). Several centuries later, the same God called Moses in the wilderness, revealing himself as Yahweh, the Lord (Exod. 3:14, 15; 6:3). The exodus deliverance from slavery in Egypt, the covenant at Sinai, and the entrance into the land of Canaan were the events through which Yahweh brought Israel into existence. A people who had been "no people" were now the people of God, with the covenant as their constitution and Yahweh as their king.

Israel's earliest written literature reflects an understanding of Yahweh as a Divine Warrior. As such, he is the one who fought against the Pharaoh of Egypt and other earthly rulers to deliver them so Israel could be his people. The Song of Deborah (Judg. 5) and the Song of Moses (Exod. 15) are ballads, celebrating the Divine Warrior's victory over those forces which threatened to destroy his people. These battles had earthly as well as cosmic repercussions; Yahweh's will was done on earth as well as in the heavens. By contrast, the ancient Near Eastern myths engaged history. For example, the Canaanite myths of the cosmic battles between Baal the storm god, and Yamm the water dragon, were never interpreted historically. But Yahweh was at work in the world as well as in the heavens to accomplish his will. There-fore, both the earthly and the cosmic arenas were places where he was active and revealing himself. The great prophets of Israel are the classical examples of those ancients who saw Yahweh's activity in both theaters.

The Root: The Prophets of Israel

The prophets of Israel combined the earthly and the heavenly dimensions in their experience and preaching. In the visions whereby they were called to be God's spokesmen, Amos and Isaiah stood in Yahweh's divine council, beheld his majesty, and heard his words (Amos 7-9; Isa. 6). The heavenly visions were given, however, so they might speak forth Yahweh's will on earth; the men of vision were also realists. As such, they stood before Israel's kings and people and declared, "Thus says the Lord, the King of Israel. . . ." Other nations were also addressed in their oracles, for Yahweh was not a mere tribal or national deity like the gods of their neighbors. The prophets of the eighth century B.C., Amos, Hosea, Micah, and Isaiah, held vision and reality together in a creative tension. They were "forthtellers" in the true sense, speaking forth, or proclaiming the will of Yahweh in the concrete circumstances of everyday life.[1]

But this balance of vision and reality became increasingly hard to maintain after Isaiah's time. There were powerful paganizing forces at work in Jerusalem and Judea in the seventh century. This was particularly true in the long reign of King Manasseh (681-642 B.C.) when Assyrian idols were set up even in the temple itself. This idolatry was countered by a reform movement during the reign of the good king Josiah (640-609 B.C.). While his reform purged the temple of heathen influences and centralized the worship in Jerusalem, there was a dangerous spirit in it insofar as it identified Israel's own national hope with Yahweh's sovereignty. The effect of this movement was to make him an ally of the nation of Israel, and thus reduce him so that he was controllable and predictable.

The events that immediately followed Josiah's reforms were disastrous for the nation of Israel. Reform had scarcely been completed when Josiah was killed by the armies of Pharaoh Necho. His successors were irresponsible rulers, caught in the trap of Egyptian, Babylonian, and Assyrian intrigues. The land was ravaged in the struggles between these great powers. The decisive blow came when Jerusalem was captured and the temple destroyed by the invading Babylonian armies (587 B.C.). The golden age had turned into a national calamity; the earlier promises of hope became echoes of despair in the book of Lamentations. Holy history turned out to be unholy history, with Yahweh's promises broken and Israel's national existence at an end. The link between the prophetic vision and the earthly reality was broken.

In this context apocalyptic ideas emerged and were first expressed within the prophetic movement of Israel. The earliest evidence of this development may be found in Ezekiel, the prophet of the exile. Though he kept the faith of the exiles in Babylon alive, there are signs in his oracles that the elements of promise and fulfillment, the structures of continuity in covenant history, were coming unraveled. Israel's past history, even in her earliest years, was interpreted by periods of tragic rebellion (Ezek. 16, 23). Only a miracle, revealed in the vision of the dry bones, would revive the dead community and give a future to the dead nation (Ezek. 37). The prophet of the late exile and return, Second Isaiah, deemphasized the past and instead put the emphasis on the new act of Yahweh in the promise of a "new exodus" from captivity when the exiles return from Babylon. "Remember not the former things nor consider the things of old. Behold, I am doing a *new thing"* (Isa. 43:18-19). And yet he kept a link with earthly realities in acknowledging Cyrus, the Persian king who released the captives, as God's chosen instrument in this return (Isa. 45:1). The new act of God became universal in scope in Isaiah 65-66, with the vision of a "new heaven and a new earth," along with the "former things" not being remembered (Isa. 65:17-25). In the concluding chapter, the prophet saw Yahweh coming in fire and in a storm chariot to judge his enemies (66:15-16). In the oracle of Zechariah 9, Yahweh, the Divine Warrior, no longer acts through human history, but leads his host alone in a universal victory over his enemies. In Zechariah 14, Yahweh goes forth alone to fight the nations whom he has gathered to do battle against Jerusalem.

These late visionary prophets, living in the postexilic period, were the early apocalyptists in Israel.[2] In the discouraging national situation, the visionaries looked beyond the harsh realities of their present situation to a future deliverance beyond the world. Salvation was described in cosmic terms and the task of relating the vision to the realities of the world was abandoned. The visionary had abandoned hope for the national and political order, trusting that Yahweh, the Divine Warrior, would win the victory without help from any human agency.

After 400 B.C., prophecy ceased in ancient Israel. The voice of the divine messenger was no longer heard in the land. The office of the prophet gave way to the priest and the cult. The elevation and preservation of the Law, inaugurated under Ezra, became the major concern. No prophet arose in Israel to interpret the meaning and significance of the conquests of Alexander the Great, to whose achievements we now turn.

The Stem: The Maccabean War

In the fourth century B.C., when the last Persian kings were poisoning and being poisoned, Philip of Macedon was dreaming of a united Greece that would dominate the world. Though he was assassinated before his ambition could be realized, his son Alexander lived to fulfill his father's dreams. Within two years after his accession to the throne in 336 B.C., he had united the Greek states into the Hellenic League. He was now ready and eager for conquering territories beyond Greece. In 334 B.C., Alexander crossed the Hellespont, and was on his way. Like a mighty tidal wave, his armies swallowed up Asia Minor, Syria, Palestine, and continued southward into Egypt. In 330 B.C., he turned his armies eastward into Persia and in a short time sealed the doom of that empire which had been the major world power for the two preceding centuries. The succeeding years found Alexander beyond the Oxus and even the Indus river. In 323 B.C., following a drunken orgy marking the funeral feast of his youth, he died of a fever. In less than thirteen years, he had conquered an area larger than that which had belonged to Persia even in her greatest days.

Aside from Alexander's military genius, his conquests are important in that they were the first stage of the Hellenization of vast areas of the conquered territory. Few men have so changed the world. He lifted the world out of one groove, and set it in another. Alexander's two great teachers were Lysimachus and Aristotle. Lysimachus, his first tutor, taught him to love the old Homeric poems and encouraged him to believe that he, Alexander, was a son of the gods. Aristotle endowed him with a great love for everything Greek and human—literature, art, language, beauty, and above all, the Greek style of government. Thus when Alexander set out to conquer the world, he was motivated by the personal ambitions that he owed to Lysimachus, as well as by the strong desire to realize those dreams of the kingdom of man which Aristotle had planted in his mind.

Alexander had a unique and effective method for Hellenizing conquered areas. When his soldiers, either due to wounds or old age, could not keep up the long forced marches that in part were the secret of his success, he discharged them in groups. These veterans settled wherever they were discharged, married native women, and raised their families. Each settlement was modeled on the Greek pattern. It was a part of Greece in a barbarian land. By these means a common culture was being established from west to east, and from north to south, and it was a Greek culture. Even with Alexander's early death, and the breakup of his empire into four parts (see Daniel 8:8, the four leaders being Cassander, Lysimachus, Seleucus, and Ptolemy), every part was Greek. Thus both the Egyptian Ptolemys, who ruled Palestine from 323-204 B.C., and the Syrian Seleucids, who ruled it after 204 B.C., were acculturated by the Hellenistic values and way of life. However, the Ptolemys were relatively tolerant, and the ancient Hebrew culture and religion was not directly threatened during their role. The Seleucids, however, were more devoted Hellenizers. This was particularly true of Antiochus IV, who became king in 175 B.C. With his ascendancy, the stage was set for a clash of cultures and religions that turned out to be the context in which Jewish apocalyptic developed into full flower.

The first round in the conflict centered around the office of the high priest in Jerusalem. It was occupied by Onias III, who was dedicated to preserving the ancient Hebrew customs. While Onias was on his way to Antioch to settle a dispute, Antiochus

IV became king. In Onias' absence, his brother Jason, who had earlier changed his Hebrew name Joshua to the Greek name Jason, offered Antiochus a large bribe for the office. Antiochus accepted, and the crafty Jason secured the office and had Onias deposed. Jason wasted no time shifting his countrymen over to the Greek way of life, introducing new customs that were contrary to the Hebrew law (see 2 Macc. 4:7-22). A gymnasium was built below the citadel, and priests hurried through their temple duties to take part in the games. Actually the process of Hellenization had made considerable headway before Jason took office, especially among the Jerusalem priests. Many Jews submitted to a surgical operation to remove the marks of circumcision. When Greek games were held at Tyre, Jason sent ambassadors with a contribution for the sacrifices to Hercules. After three years the tables were turned on Jason when he lost his office to a still higher bidder, Menelaus (2 Macc. 4:22-50). The orthodox had detested Jason, but he was at least a member of the high-priestly family. Menelaus had no such pedigree. Furthermore, he was totally unscrupulous. He arranged to have the former high priest Onias murdered; then he had his brother, Lysimachus, steal the holy vessels in the temple. The Jews were enraged at these actions; violence followed in which the temple robber was killed. The corruption of the high priestly office and its consequent decline is an important element in the climate which is the background to Jewish apocalyptic. Serious and devout Jews became disenchanted with the office, and even with the whole temple cult. Some of these dissenters formed the Qumran community—having left Jerusalem and the corrupted worship of the temple institution, they went out into the Judean wilderness to "prepare the way of the Lord."

The second round of the conflict involved a much larger segment of the Jewish population. Greek culture had been penetrating Palestine peacefully for decades, but Antiochus IV was determined to complete the process and make the Jews into Greeks. His purpose was to unify "his whole kingdom (so) that all should be one people, and that each should give up his kingdom" (1 Macc. 1:41). He issued letters to his messengers in Jerusalem and the cities of Judea which prohibited the offerings and sacrifices in the temple sanctuary. Possession of copies of the law was made a capital offense. Circumcision was forbidden, and mothers and families who had their sons circumcised were put to death. Pressures were put on the Jews to eat unclean foods and to neglect the Sabbath worship. The language and customs of their fathers were to be forsaken in favor of Greek customs. Altars and shrines to Greek deities were built and Jews were ordered to sacrifice at these worship centers. The climax was Antiochus' erection of an image to Zeus upon the altar of burnt offerings in the temple on 15 Chislev, 167 B.C., and the offering of a sow upon it on 25 Chislev, 167 B.C. It is significant that the historian who wrote 1 Maccabees dated the events (1 Macc. 1:54, 59; cf. also 2 Macc. 6:1-6). For him, these abominable acts were the crowning outrage of Antiochus' program. Antiochus correctly understood that the heart of the opposition to him was of a religious character, so he sought to stamp out the Jewish religion. He regarded himself as the visible "appearance" of the Olympian Zeus, so he became known as Antiochus "Epiphanes." However, his enemies renamed him Antiochus "Epimanes," meaning "the madman."

Faithful Jews resisted these repressive and idolatrous measures. At first it was a passive resistance, but soon the opposition broke out in open revolt and guerilla warfare. Antiochus' officers tried to enforce the pagan worship at Modein, a town northwest of Jerusalem, but the village priest, Mattathias, refused to sacrifice. When a Jew came forward to offer the sacrifice, Mattathias ran a sword through him and the king's officer, and then called his sons and others who were zealous for the Law and the covenant to come with him to the hills. There they were joined by many other nationalistic Jews, and even by the Hasideans, the "pious ones" (1 Macc. 2:42). This group, which was motivated primarily by religious concern for the Law, had first resisted passively but now joined the militants in resisting force with force. Together they organized an army which struck at Jews cooperating with the Gentiles, tore down heathen altars, and even forcibly circumcised boys in Israel. When Mattathias died, he was succeeded by Judas, the third of his five sons. He earned his nickname, Maccabeus, "the Hammerer," in the many battles so vividly described in 1 Maccabees. Led by the stout-hearted Judas, the inspired fighters captured a major portion of Jerusalem, including the temple. The temple was purified and decorated with new furnishings. The defiled altar was demolished and a new one built. On 25 Chislev 164 B.C., three years to the day after Antiochus had offered a pagan sacrifice, Judas and his army, together with blameless priests, solemnly offered sacrifice according to the law on the new altar of burnt offering (1 Macc. 4:52-59). The joyous service went on for eight days, with Judas decreeing that the days of celebration be observed for future generations, beginning with 25 Chislev each year. The Jewish Hanukkah festival still commemorates this heroic and happy occasion.

The main supporters of the Maccabean revolt in the early years were men of strong religious convictions. They fought in the ancient tradition of the holy war, as zealous warriors fighting the battle of the Lord. The persecutions of Antiochus seemed to them to be the final days of trial before the Lord would prevail and bring in his kingdom. The joyous rededication of the temple and resumption of the sacrifice was a necessary preliminary to this coming rule of God. The Maccabean war continued for many years, and eventually became more and more a political war. It finally resulted in an independent Jewish kingdom, with later Maccabeans, or Hasmoneans on the throne, but it also divided the Jews into separate parties and sects which still existed at the time of Christ.

The corruption of the high priestly office and the Maccabean war were the key events in the intertestamental period. The Jews never forgot Antiochus Epiphanes; he remained the symbol of evil and a type of the one who would come before the final messianic age. The struggle against him had been costly and many of the faithful had perished. These harsh realities of history raised serious questions for devout Jews who believed in a just and living God. What would be the reward of the righteous, especially those who died professing the faith? What would be the religious worth of their sacrifice?

The Flower: The Sufferings of the Righteous

The primary sources for a knowledge of this period are the two books of the Maccabees, which belong to the Apocrypha and are therefore not familiar to most Protestants. This ignorance is unfortunate. Not only do the books of the Maccabees have much historical value, but their heroes, especially the martyrs, are thrilling examples of faithfulness and endurance in the face of persecution. These righteous ones are the full flowering of Jewish piety and loyalty in the intertestamental period. They have been an inspiration to both Jews and Christians.

1 Maccabees was probably written about 130 B.C., and the author may have been an eyewitness to some of the events during the struggle with Antiochus Epiphanes. The unnamed author was a very good historian. He wrote with a great deal of

restraint, only rarely showing his own opinions. He knew the geography of Palestine very well. The central figures in his account are the Maccabees, or members of the Hasmonean family, "through whom deliverance was granted to Israel" (5:62). Though he suggests that their success as military leaders was due to divine help, he does not say that they were divinely ordained for their task. He prefers to use the term "heaven" when speaking of God, reflecting the transcendent view which so many Jews of that time had concerning the Almighty.

2 Maccabees is a summary of a five-volume work written by a certain Jason of Cyrene. 2 Maccabees was written in Greek in one of the lands of the dispersion, probably in Alexandria late in the second century B.C. The author's purpose was to edify and stir up the Jews to religious unity. It has been called "pathetic history" because the story which the author tells is filled with such pathos and drama (RSV Annotated Bible with Apocrypha, Oxford, xi). The language is colorful and picturesque; the book is full of fiery arguments and invectives against the enemies of the Jews. Miracles get a very prominent place in 2 Maccabees, with frequent mention of angels. While this makes for more interesting reading, 2 Maccabees is not nearly as accurate and historically reliable as 1 Maccabees. The author's basic theme is that the sin of the nation is the cause of the divine punishment (4:17). The Lord sends suffering to discipline the people, but not to destroy them. The sufferings are a warning to people to repent, but also a sign of the Lord's kindness which should encourage them to steadfastness in sufferings.

2 Maccabees 6-7 narrates two examples of steadfast suffering in the midst of persecution. They are the stories of Eleazar and the Jewish mother and her seven sons, all of whom suffered during the terror under Antiochus Epiphanes. Eleazar, a ninety-year-old scribe, was forced to eat swine's flesh. But he spit out

the meat, preferring death with honor rather than life with pollution, and went up to the rack of his own accord (6:19). The authorities tried to reason with him, but he rejected their suggestions. While he was dying from their blows, he gave a speech: "It is clear to the Lord in his holy knowledge that, though I might have been saved from death, I am enduring terrible sufferings in my body under this beating, but in my soul I am glad to suffer these things because I fear him." (6:30). The mother and her seven sons were also commanded to eat pork. They also refused, preferring to die rather than break the laws of their fathers. The enraged king ordered that the pans and caldrons be heated, and the first son was brought out and dismembered while the rest of the family looked on, encouraging one another to die nobly. One by one, the sons were brought forth, tortured and put to death, while the mother encouraged each to be steadfast to the end. Antiochus offered a large bribe to the last son to turn him from the ways of his fathers, but to no avail. The king then called upon the mother to save her last son. But she, speaking to her son in Hebrew, urged him to "accept death so that in God's mercy I may get you back again with your brothers" (7:29). Then the last son and also the mother were put to death.

These stories are told in even greater detail in 4 Maccabees, which comes from the first century A.D. This writing does not even mention the Maccabean warriors, but tells the heroic deaths of Eleazar and the mother and her seven sons in great detail. The story of the mother, who is given the name Hannah, and her sons is in fact the principal subject of 4 Maccabees. The book is a Jewish martyrology. Some of the details came from 2 Maccabees 6-7, but others from the author's imagination. In spite of all his interest in the stories, he was influenced by Hellenistic Stoicism; he saw the martyrs as people who used pious reason to control passion.

Another example of how such heroism was glorified may be found in the apocalyptic work, the Assumption of Moses. This, too, was written in the first century A.D. Again there is no mention of the Maccabean warriors. Chapter 9 is a redactional work that combines the two martyr stories of 2 Maccabees 6 (Eleazar) and 7 (the seven brothers, sons of the widow). In this work the hero is a man of the tribe of Levi whose name is Taxo. He exhorted his seven sons to fast for three days and on the fourth day to go into a cave and die rather than transgress the commands of the Lord (9:7). F. C. Burkitt and R. H. Charles, scholars of apocalyptic literature, conclude that Taxo refers to Eleazar.[3] This version serves an important interpretive purpose. The author intentionally has avoided referring to Mattathias who had five sons. By implication he is censuring the Maccabean uprising with its use of force and weapons. His sympathies are with the nonviolent and quietistic among the Hasidim, and in particular with those who accepted death for their convictions, trusting that the Lord would vindicate them. In the Assumption of Moses, the ideal is not "Let us war," but "Let us die rather than transgress." Charles regards the author as a quietistic Pharisee whose views were rooted in Old Testament concepts of God's justice and final vindication of right and wrong.

Several important conclusions may be drawn from this study of the beginnings of apocalyptic in Judaism.

First, there was a tremendous loyalty to the will of God as revealed in the Covenant and the Law. The knowledge that they were called to be God's people was the common denominator in the conviction of the earlier prophet and the suffering righteous Jews of the Maccabean period. This gave them an identity and set them apart from the Gentiles. It governed the way they lived their lives. Total loyalty to the Lord and his Law was required.

Their stubbornness seemed like "sheer madness" to the authorities (2 Macc. 6:29). But no deviations from the Law were possible, especially if these could be regarded as assenting to heathen idolatry. Both prophet and Maccabean hero drew upon roots which were hundreds of years old, the Mosaic Covenant and Law.

Second, there was a clear and discernible shift from the earlier holy war concepts toward a passive, nonviolent resistance of the enemy. Eleazar, for example, went willingly to the torture rack without appealing to arms. God's judgment of the tormentors would be sufficient retribution. Even in 1 Maccabees there is the account of the massacre of the pious Jewish refugees who refused to fight on the Sabbath. "Let us all die in our innocence; heaven and earth testify for us that you are killing us unjustly" (1 Macc. 2:37). For the devout Jew, as well as for his later Christian descendent, the emphasis lay on suffering rather than armed opposition.

Third, the righteous who suffered were representatives of the whole people of Israel. Eleazar died, "leaving in his death an example of nobility and a memorial of courage, not only to the young but to the great body of his nation" (2 Macc. 6:31). In the more developed tradition of 4 Maccabees, he died with the words: "Be merciful unto thy people, and let our punishment be a satisfaction in their behalf. Make my blood their purification, and take my soul to ransom their souls" (6:28f.). The last of the seven brothers gave up his life as a sacrifice on behalf of his people, and to bring to an end the wrath of the Almighty that had fallen on the nation of Israel (2 Macc. 7:38-39). Persecution was the result of sin, and suffering was its expiation. The persecution would end after the sacrifice was made and the cleansing completed.

Finally, the suffering and sacrifice of the righteous for the nation was a preparation for the age to come. Their suffering was eschatological. The conflict between the seven and the foreign power that persecuted them was regarded as a battle between God and his adversaries, with the suffering of the righteous, who are God's representatives, as the means by which people are delivered from condemnation (2 Macc. 7:32f.). While God was not to deliver his people immediately, he would in the near future, when Antiochus Epiphanes was to be repaid in full (7:17), and the sufferers rewarded. When the fourth son was near death, he said to the king: "One cannot but choose to die at the hands of men and to cherish the hope that God gives of being raised again by him. But for you there will be no resurrection to life!" (7:14). And the mother nobly encouraged her sons by words of resurrection hope: "It was not I who gave you life and breath, nor I who set in order the elements within each of you. Therefore the Creator of the world who shaped the beginning of man and devised the origin of all things, will in his mercy give life and breath back to you again, since you now forget yourselves for the sake of his laws" (7:22-23).

The sufferings of the righteous and the traditions that interpreted their devotion are the flowering of late Judaism. It is not surprising that their heroism was remembered by later Christian martyrs. Both the Eastern and Western churches dedicated a Commemoration Day to the "Maccabean Saints," Hannah and her seven sons.

An
3 Old Testament
Apocalypse:
The Book of Daniel

The Book of Daniel is the only apocalypse in the Old Testament. In the classification of books in the Christian Bible, Daniel has been placed with the Prophets, right after the prophet of the exile, Ezekiel. At the first reading this would seem in the right sequence, for the author appears to be living in the time of Nebuchadnezzar in the sixth century B.C., and predicting events from then to the time of the Maccabees about 165 B.C. This has been the traditional interpretation and it is still held by some biblical scholars although rejected by the majority of others. It is therefore necessary to deal first with the questions of authorship and date before interpreting the book itself.

Who was the author of this book? The book is about Daniel, although he is not explicitly stated to be the author. The name Daniel means "God has given a decision." We have very little information from Judaism about any Daniel except from this book. Ezekiel wrote about three men, Noah, Daniel, and Job, whom he considered righteous (14:14); further, the Lord spoke to the prince of Tyre: "You are indeed wiser than Daniel" (28:3). Yet the Daniel of Ezekiel was not a man from the time of the exile. A poem discovered at Ras Shamra, Syria, in 1929 was about a King Danel who defended the rights of the widow and orphan at the time of the Babylonian captivity; his righteousness invited divine action that brought reward and triumph for those Jews that remained loyal to the Law. It is dubious, however, to link this King Danel with the biblical Daniel, and to conclude that a Jewish legend in a Canaanite text gives us direct supporting evidence for sixth century Danielic authorship. It would seem, though, that Daniel was a man of considerable authority in Jewish circles in order to have an apocalypse named after him, but the sketchy evidence just cited does not show this.

A close examination of the external and internal evidence raises serious questions about the traditional sixth century dating and authorship. What are some of the facts on this issue? We begin with the external evidence.

The Book of Daniel is not found among the body of prophetic books in the Hebrew Bible. Instead, it is placed among the Writings—the third major class of books in the Hebrew Bible. Daniel was added to the Writings in A.D. 90, when the canon of the Hebrew Bible was completed at the Council of Jamnia. Thus Daniel's position in the Christian Bible among the regular Old Testament prophets is not consistent with the original Hebrew order.

The Book of Daniel was not referred to in any Jewish literature until after 150 B.C., when the books of 1 Maccabees and the Jewish apolcalyptic book of the Sibylline Oracles (3:397-400) mentioned it. The apocryphal book of Ecclesiasticus, written about 190 B.C. by Jesus ben Sirach, made a list of great Jewish men down to his own time (Ecclus. 44:1–50:24). He included the names of exilic and post-exilic figures, among them the twelve prophets, Zerubbabel, Nehemiah, and Simon, a high priest about 200 B.C., but Daniel was not included.

The internal evidence from the book itself raises more questions about the traditional date. A large section, Daniel 2:4b–7:28 was written in Aramaic, but this language was not popular among the Jews until well after the exile; by the second century it had become the common spoken language of Jews in Palestine. The Hebrew in the book is similar to the Hebrew of late books like Ecclesiastes and Esther. There are words in Daniel that definitely come from Persian and Greek languages, which is further evidence for dating after the sixth century.

Theologically, the place and function of angels in the book was not the typical Jewish view of the sixth century B.C. In the visions of the classical prophets God himself gave the interpretation (Amos 7–9; Isa. 6; Jer. 1). In Ezekiel, which was written in the transitional era of the sixth century, both God and an angel discharged the office of interpretation. But in Daniel, it is an angel who gives the interpretation, and this is also true of apocalyptic works such as 1 Enoch, Testaments of the Twelve Patriarchs, Book of Jubilees, 2 Baruch, and 2 Esdras. This is a characteristic of late Judaism's shift to a highly transcendent view of the Almighty, with the great distance between God and man bridged by angels. Only in this book of the Old Testament, for example, do we read about the "watchers," though again they are frequently mentioned in other Jewish apocalyptic writings.

Finally, in literary form and content the Book of Daniel is an apocalypse. The author is a visionary who *reinterprets* history, with much allegorizing, from the time of Nebuchadnezzar down to Antiochus Epiphanes and the Maccabees. He summarizes this period in four world ages, with humanity now living in the fourth and last epoch, which will be followed by the kingdom of God. The vision and descriptions in Daniel, especially in Chapter 7, are cosmic in scope. As a literary form, it is an apocalypse, similar in this respect to the apocalyptic visions in 1 Enoch 85–90, 2 Baruch 53, and the seven visions of 2 Esdras. All of these writings undeniably come from the second century B.C. or later.

On the weight of such evidence, both internal and external, I suggest that the traditional view of the sixth century authorship should be abandoned. Simply repeating a traditional idea in the face of strong evidence to the contrary does not make the idea true and the evidence presented above suggests a later date, probably in the second century B.C., for the writing of the present Book of Daniel. The author may well have drawn upon traditions from an earlier period for his book, reworking them into a treatise for his own time. If the hypothesis that he wrote during the time of the Maccabean war is correct, the Book of Daniel reflects a time of intense persecution.

What kind of man was the author? Why did he write the book? The Book of Daniel reveals an author of great vision and faith. Perhaps he was one of the Hasidim. He was also a man of great literary ability, who used stories and numbers and allegories in a creative and powerful way to tell his message. He obviously wrote to strengthen people in their faith and loyalty to God. The author shares with his people their awful distress and persecution, but he is convinced that God will be victorious. His message to his people is this: *Hold fast to God in your trials, and he will bring you through in the end*. This is repeated again and again in each story and dream-vision throughout the book.

The Stories of Daniel (Chapters 1–6)

The first six chapters consist of stories that focus on the adventures of four young Jews, God's servants in a foreign land. The literary genre of story rather than history is more applicable to these chapters. The stories are based on Jewish traditions that were probably told and retold for generations before being committed to writing. The personalities and events have a basis in fact, though they have been reinterpreted by the writer, hereafter referred to as Daniel, to apply to his own time and situation.

The six stories have their setting in the Babylonian exile of the Jews in the sixth century B.C. They are written in the narrative style, with the exception of four doxologies to Israel's God that interrupt the narrative (Dan. 2:20-23; 4:3; 4:34b-35; 6:26b-27). The central figure in the stories is Daniel, who is written about in the third person in this section. He and his three fellow Jews, Hananiah, Mishael, and Azariah, are given Babylonian names, Belteshazzar, Shadrach, Meshach, and Abednego (cf. 1:6-7). Name giving was a sign of authority among the ancients, though the incident passes without comment in the text. Many Jews in Babylon changed their names at this time, just as many European immigrants did when they came to America. There is no hint in Daniel that this practice was regarded as wrong, but the name Belteshazzar is used in only eight verses while Daniel is used over seventy times.

The king's court confronted Daniel and his friends with temptations and dangers. They were told to eat unclean food (chap. 1), to worship an idol (chap. 3), and to pray to the king (chap. 6). The young men, represented here as ideal Jews, refuse to obey, and their God delivers them in each of these dangers. The author was urging his readers, who were facing similar dangers and temptations, to trust that God would also deliver them.

The king's court also presented Daniel with opportunities. The dangerous situation became an occasion for proclaiming the true God of Israel in a heathen environment. This confrontation of the demands of the heathen court with the claims of the true God constitutes the plot of these chapters. The drama of this encounter is developed in various ways, but the most subtle and profound form is through dreams and their interpretation. It is precisely through his God-given ability to interpret dreams that Daniel achieves prominence and power in a foreign court.

Ancient peoples—and many moderns too—were fascinated with dreams. They regarded them as revelations of supernatural events. Dreams were divine communications, and seers (interpreters of dreams) were held in high regard because they were links with the divine. Furthermore, what was dreamed might later actually happen; the interpreters of dreams thus held the key to unlock the future. In Babylon the seers were known as the *baru,* and they studied dreams with great attention to detail. They even wrote Dream Books, which were later included in Ashurbanipal's library at ancient Nineveh. They had a goddess of dreams, named Mahir; a small temple to this goddess has been discovered in modern times near Mosul, Iraq. This was the setting in which Daniel had to live, and the *baru* made up the court with which he had to contend!

Like Joseph centuries before him, Daniel was called on to interpret dreams in a foreign court. These are the only examples in the Old Testament where Jews interpreted dreams; revelation through a vision was the usual means whereby God revealed his will. Daniel is indeed very similar in form to the story of Joseph in Genesis 41. Daniel and his three fellow Jews, all ideal Israelites, are found competent to serve in the king's palace. They are willing to serve in the court, but refuse the king's rich food and drink, living instead on simple natural vegetables (cf. 2 Macc. 5:27). God gives them wisdom so that at the end of their training period, they are found to be "ten times better" than all the Babylonian enchanters and magicians (1:20).

Thus they succeed where the court seers failed. The story of

Daniel 2 contrasts the feebleness of human wisdom with that conferred by God. Nebuchadnezzar had a dream, which the seers could not reproduce, even with the aid of dream books. In their estimation Daniel is able to do that which only the gods could do because God had revealed the mystery to him. He had been in the royal council where the "deep and mysterious things" were revealed to him. Therefore, he is able to make the dream's interpretation known to the king (2:36-45). The climax comes with the explanation of the stone, not made with hands, shattering the four earthly kingdoms and then filling the whole earth. The everlasting kingdom of God will come as a successor to the kingdoms of the world. This dream then fulfills the line in the hymn: "He changes times and seasons; he removes kings and sets up kings" (2:21).

Daniel 4 is another story that develops this same theme. Nebuchadnezzar, on a worldwide ego-trip, issues a grandiose and extravagant decree (4:1ff.). But he has still another dream which alarms him. Again the wise men of Babylon are called to interpret it, but without success. Daniel is called, coming at just the right psychological moment. Even he is alarmed at the dream, but he finally gives the king the grim interpretation: the huge tree that will be reduced to a stump "is you, O king" (4:22). And the mighty Nebuchadnezzar, at the pinnacle of success, is reduced for a time to the level of a beast that eats the grass of the field. As soon as he recognizes God's ultimate sovereignty (4:34-35), his sanity and the relative right of his own sovereignty is restored.

The same theme is continued in Chapter 5, with some of the details changed. King Belshazzar gives a tremendous banquet. While the feast is in progress, he orders the gold and silver vessels from the temple of Jerusalem to be brought into the feast. The feast probably had a cultic, even an orgiastic character to it, so the use of the sacred vessels in connection with the heathen worship would be a terrible blasphemy to a devout Jew. Belshazzar's drinking bout is interrupted by a hand writing on the wall. The king, pale and trembling, calls the court wizards, but they cannot interpret the message. Then Daniel is brought in. He is given a friendly greeting by the king, and promised high honors and power (cf. Gen. 41:40-43). But Daniel brusquely dismisses this talk, quite in contrast to his earlier courteous attitude toward Nebuchadnezzar. Two more gifts, the ability to explain riddles and to solve problems (5:12, 16), have now been added to his abilities. After sternly rebuking the monarch, Daniel interprets the writing. Its meaning is grim and final: "He has numbered! He has weighed! He has divided! The Persians!" (Bauer). Belshazzar is weighed in the balance scales of God, who uses strict justice as his standard of measurement, and is found wanting. That very night he is killed by the invading Persians.

Chapters 3 and 6 are parallel stories in theme, development and final result. In Chapter 3, Shadrach, Meschach and Abednego are cast into the fiery furnace for refusing to worship Nebuchadnezzar's golden image. Similarly, in Chapter 6 Daniel is thrown into the lion's den for defying Darius' irrevocable decree that forbade prayer to anyone other than the king himself for thirty days. The stories also have a similar background—the context of heathen environment and the pressures to pagan idolatry, encouraged and abetted by the flattering hordes of advisers that surrounded the oriental monarch in his royal court. In each instance, too, God's servants are miraculously delivered unharmed as a result of divine intervention. Shadrach, Meshach, and Abednego are joined by a fourth figure, later called an angel, whose appearance was like a son of the gods; Daniel is saved because God sends an angel that shuts the lion's mouth. The men who threw Shadrach, Meshach, and Abednego into the furnace are themselves killed by the flames; likewise Daniel's accusers, together with their families, are thrown into the den and killed by the lions. The *jus talionis* was put into effect, consistent with the treatment of a false witness in the Law: "You shall do to him as he had meant to do to his brother" (Deut. 19:16-19). The basic lesson of these stories was to encourage the faithful to be steadfast even in the face of death, trusting that God would be with them and deliver his servants. These stories are powerfully and skillfully told. It is interesting that they are best known to modern people through Negro spirituals, whose authors found a common wavelength with which they could identify and reinterpret the message through music.

The same message runs through all six chapters. Daniel and his three fellow Jews worship and serve the God whose rule is everlasting, whose kingdom shall never be destroyed, and whose sovereignty shall not be left to another people (2:44). In fact, his superiority over against every earthly authority is affirmed in every chapter and story (see esp. 1:17-19; 2:21, 46ff.; 3:29; 4:37; 5:21ff.; 6:26ff.). All earthly authority of ruling kings and monarchs is a derived authority, because God has given it to them for a limited time (see 2:37-38; 4:17, 32; 5:18ff.), and they are finally accountable to him. Therefore, even Nebuchadnezzar and Darius, kings of Babylon and Persia, acknowledge his authority. He deals justly with all human pride and power that oversteps human boundaries, humbling Nebuchadnezzar and destroying Belshazzar. He reveals the deep mysteries of his will to Daniel, his servant, who through interpretation of dreams confounds the human wisdom of the seers in the most sophisticated royal courts of the day. Human pride and pretension have their limits because God has set the boundaries and limits to them. Therefore, trust him and hold fast to your faith for he will deliver you!

The Dream-visions of Daniel (Chapters 7–12)

The stories in Daniel 1–6 have shown how futile human kingdoms are in opposing God. These kingdoms have almost run their course in history, their days are numbered, and *now* God's *final* intervention is at hand. This is the theme of the dream-visions in Daniel 7–12.

Although Daniel continues to be the hero in these chapters, there is an important difference. In the stories he interpreted the visions; now he is the recipient of dreams and visions. This brings a change in literary style. The stories, written in the third person, told us about Daniel; in the dream-visions, written in the first person, Daniel himself is the speaker. The only exceptions are 7:1 and 10:1, which are connective and were obviously added by the redactor.

All of the visions are dated. Carefully stating the time and place of a dream or a vision was a feature of Jewish apocalyptic. The dream-vision is dated in the first year of Belshazzar (7:1), while the other visions are dated in the third year of Belshazzar (8:1-2), the first year of Darius (9:1-2), and the third year of Cyrus (10:1). The structure of the chapters is as follows:

Prologue:	The Vision:	The Interpretation:	Epilogue:
7:1	7:2-4 *	7:17-27	7:28
8:1-2	8:3-12 *	8:15-25	8:26-27
9:1-19	9:2-23	9:24-27	
10:1-4	10:5-21	11:1–12:4	12:5-13

* 7:15-16, Daniel's distress; 8:13-14, a celestial prediction.

The visions fill out the historical sketch of Nebuchadnezzar's dream (Dan. 2). All four visions have the same horizon. They lead history up to the same point, which is the great tribulation that just precedes the end.

In the dream-vision of Chapter 7, there are four beasts, just as there were four metals in Chapter 2. Though all rise out of the sea, each one differs from the other. The standard by which they are judged is their treatment of the Jews, the people of God. Whom do these beasts represent? There are various answers, although the most widely accepted view is that of H. H. Rowley who suggests that they represented the Babylonian, Median, Persian, and Greek-Macedonian empires.[1] His suggestions seem best in fitting the historical facts together.

The winged-lion is an appropriate description of Babylon. This creature was very common in Babylonian art, though used by other cultures as well. In the Old Testament, the winged-lion was a symbol for Nebuchadnezzar (Jer. 50:44). Its wings were plucked when it was shorn of its power by Cyrus. Then this creature, once so proud and fearless, was reduced to a state of feebleness and dependency.

The kingdom of the Medes is represented by a bear, which is inferior to the lion. The bear does not play a large role in biblical symbolism, though it was regarded as a ferocious animal that aroused great dread (Isa. 21:2ff.). The leopard with four wings and four heads represents Persia. The four wings seem to refer to the rapid conquests that they made under Cyrus (Isa. 41:3); the four heads probably refer to the four Persian kings that were familiar to the Jews, namely, Cyrus, Xerxes, Artaxerxes, and Darius.

The fourth animal is a terrible monster that cannot be classified by any zoologist. This awful creature has destructive functions: to devour with teeth of iron, to crush with his front feet, and to trample with his hind feet. The ten horns on the creature's head represent ten kings (cf. Dan. 2:41-42). The exact identity of these kings is not clear, although the Sibylline Oracles (3:381-400), which were written only a generation later than Daniel, referred them to individuals in the Seleucid line. As Daniel observes the horns, he notices a little horn sprouting which shoves aside three other horns to make room for itself. The reference is to Antiochus' taking the throne for himself, which historically was the case. But Daniel is careful to point out that the little horn was a human and not a divine being.

While Daniel stares at the little horn and listens to its loud-mouthed talk, his gaze shifts from earth to heaven (7:9ff.). In a vision he sees the Ancient of Days getting his heavenly court ready to judge the nations. The monster is killed in the heavenly vision, implying that a similar judgment upon the earth is imminent. The other three beasts get a reprieve, perhaps that they might be vassals to the saints of the Most High, and be absorbed in the final kingdom. God then gives an everlasting dominion to "one like a son of man" who has come with the clouds of heaven (7:13-14). This "one like a son of man" is a heavenly being who receives the kingdom on behalf of the heavenly host which he leads and also on behalf of his earthly subjects, the faithful of Israel in the latter age.

This strange heavenly vision is interpreted in 7:17-27. Daniel contrasts the earthly kingdoms with the heavenly kingdom, the beasts that come from below with the kingdom that comes from above. The kingdom will be given to the "saints of the Most High," the godly ones in the era of persecution of this last age. Daniel shows a special fascination with the fourth beast, and he again inquires about it. In the reply (7:23-27), the description of the beast is repeated and enlarged from that of 7:7-9. He is not referred to again as the "little horn," but as one who shall exercise vast powers on earth with destructive results, and who "shall speak words against the Most High, and shall wear out the saints of the Most High, and shall think to change the times and the law: and they shall be given into his hand for a time, two times, and half a time" (7:25). This is Daniel's way of saying that this earthly tyrant's days are numbered. For the ancient Jew, a time, two times, and half a time, or 3½, was half the divine number of seven (cf. Dan. 4:16, 9:27). (It is somewhat similar to the term "half-a-dozen" in our language). It would not be long before God would deal with this king, this tyrant, and show him who really was King. His message to the suffering faithful on earth is to trust and take courage and to look to the future, for the present sufferings are under God's control!

Having thus assured his readers, Daniel turns to the question, "*How long* will the persecution last"? The answer is given in the three visions that follow (chapters 8-12).

The vision of the two-horned ram and the he-goat is a sketch of history from the Medo-Persian empire to the time of Antiochus. It reads somewhat like a political cartoon. The ram's aggressive behavior depicts the campaigns of the Medes and the Persians; he butts his way to conquests in the west, north, and south. The he-goat was a symbol of power and leadership (cf. Isa. 14:9 and Zech. 10:3, where it is used of princes). His rapid victories and far-flung conquests are summarized in a picturesque way by stating that he moved "across the face of the whole earth, without touching the ground" (8:5). His attack on the ram and the ram's total defeat depict the collapse of the Persian empire to Alexander (8:6-7; cf. 1 Macc. 1:1-4). Then at the height of his power, the great horn was broken with Alexander's death in 323 B.C., and the kingdom divided, with four other horns coming up in its place. In the remainder of the vision Daniel concentrates on the actions and threats of the "little horn" who is obviously Antiochus Epiphanes (8:9-14). His arrogant actions challenge God and the heavenly host; God himself was chal-

lenged when the offering that was his due, the burnt offering of
the evening and morning sacrifice as prescribed in the Torah,
was stopped (Exod. 29:38ff.; Num. 28:3ff.). Any outside inter-
ference with the worship of Yahweh or neglect by the worshipers themselves was considered a dreadful disaster to the devout Jew (see 1 Macc. 4:38-39). The answer to the question of
the holy one, "How long?" is given in the colloquy of the two
angels in 8:13-14. It will be 2300 evenings and mornings before
the sanctuary will be cleansed and restored. Paraphrased in the
language of our Christian liturgy, this would read: "It will be
2300 evening matins and morning suffrages," or 1150 days. This
assurance may have had its clue from Zech. 1:9-12, where the
prophet has done some eavesdropping on a conversation between
two angels.

The remainder of the chapter involves the interpretation of
the vision by the angel Gabriel, the angel of revelation. The interpretation is generally self-explanatory. When he comes to Antiochus he sketches in more details. He portrays him as a crafty
figure; "one who understands riddles" could have the meaning
of "a master of intrigue" (8:23). Thus Antiochus is viewed as
skilled in double-dealing and deceit, but when he attacks the
Almighty One he overextends himself. His power is to be broken
without any human agency (8:25, cf. also 2:34 and 11:45, 2 Macc.
9:5, and Josephus, *Ant.* XII. 9.1). Then Daniel is told to "seal up
the vision" (8:26). Keep it secret! The end may not be far off,
but it is not yet.

Except for the dating, the prolog in Chapter 9 consists of Daniel's prayer (9:3-19). Several commentators have referred to it as
the "Kyrie eleison" of the Old Testament (Heaton, Porteous
et al).[2] It breathes a spirit of deep loyalty to the ancestral faith
nourished among the people; this is the voice of Hasidim. The
personal name of Yahweh is used only in this chapter in the

book. The prayer follows a liturgical style; its spirit is thoroughly penitential. The long confession could appropriately be summarized, "Thine is the right, ours is the shame." It is a shame in which all share—kings and princes, family houses and commoners. It has been accurately observed that people get the kind of politicians and leaders they deserve. Because of their shame, a great calamity has come upon Israel. The prayer closes with a plea that Yahweh will forgive and hear and act; the plea is based solely on God's mercy, not on the merit of the people for whom the prayer is said.

The vision that follows deals again with the question, "How long?" (9:20-27). The answer is given in the seventy weeks of years (cf. Jer. 25:12-14; 29:10-14) which is subdivided into periods of seven, sixty-two, and one. The first seven weeks begin with the proclamation of God and the coming of an anointed prince; the next sixty-two concern the building of the city; the last week is the time of catastrophe, when an anointed one is cut off, an army comes and destroys the city and sanctuary, and war makes everything desolate (cf. 1. Macc. 1:11-15, 54; 4:52ff.). The main purpose is to demonstrate the nearness of the deliverance from the tyranny of Antiochus; they are on the threshold of a new age. When the seventy weeks of years (490 years) are reconstructed, the following chronology emerges:

1. seven weeks = 49 years, from 587-538 (Dan. 9:25: from Jerusalem's destruction to the decree of Cyrus, Ezra 1:1-4, 6:3-5);

2. sixty-two weeks = 434 years, from 605-171 (Dan. 9:25b-26: from the time of the first exiles to Antiochus);

3. one week = 7 years, from 171-164 (Dan. 9:27):

a. one-half week = 3½ years, from 171-167—high priest Onias is deposed, war begins;

b. one-half week = 3½ years, from 167-164—abomination of the temple, sacrifices and offerings cease (for a time!).

Some Christians, however, reading Daniel as predictive prophecy, have reckoned the decree from the time of Ezra. In 457 B.C. the scribe Ezra left Babylon, with the permission of King Artaxerxes, to promote a reform in Judah and make the Law the charter of her existence (Ezra 7:7-8). An alternate chronology results from this dating and computation:

1. seven and sixty-two weeks = 483 years, from 457 B.C. to A.D. 26 (Dan. 9:25-26: from the time of Ezra to Christ beginning his ministry);

2. one week = 7 years, from A.D. 26-33 (Dan. 9:27: for half of the week he causes sacrifice and offering to cease with the sacrifice on the cross).

This alternative interpretation starts with a less important king and decree, however. Cyrus, the Lord's "anointed" (cf. Isa. 45:1), surely outweighs Artaxerxes in Israel's historical significance, even as his decree to rebuild the temple was of much more importance than the one later issued by Artaxerxes to Ezra.

Chapters 10–12 consist of an angelic vision of the last days with an interpretation given by an unnamed angel, probably Gabriel. The vision experience had an even more profound effect on Daniel than the previous ones; it left him on the ground, dazed. The numinous character of the experience is further heightened by the fact that those men who were with him, though they did not see what he saw, were seized with panic and left him alone. When Daniel is revived by the touch of a mysterious hand, the angel explains that he had been delayed for three weeks in coming with the interpretation because he was also the guardian angel of the prince of Persia and that prince was slow to heed his guardian's advice. Only Michael's intervention had freed him. Behind this strange passage is the idea that the fortunes of the earthly nations are dependent on what happens in the heavenly sphere. This exalted view of angels and their power to effect events on earth was characteristic of late Jewish apocalyptic thought.

The interpretation itself covers several centuries of history (11:2ff.). In a few verses the angelic messenger briefly explains the rise and fall of Persia and Alexander's empire, and then gives a longer discourse on the kings of the south and the north, the Ptolemies and the Seleucids. This takes him down to his main subject, Antiochus (11:21-45), whom he characterizes as "a contemptible person" who grabbed an authority not rightfully his. His persecution of the Jews, deposing the "prince of the covenant" (Onias III), and setting up "the abomination that makes desolate" (11:31) effects a division among them. Some shall be seduced by his flattery (cf. 1 Macc. 2:18), but others, "know their God shall stand firm and take action" (11:32). Heaton properly renders this verse as "the people that *know* their God shall be strong, and *do*." Religious persecution then divides the sheep from the goats. The faithful are the "wise" among the people; this likely refers to the Hasidim, who looked for deliverance from the Lord and not from man's efforts (cf. 3:17). Daniel acknowledges only that they receive a "little help" from the Maccabees, whose actions had drawn a mixed crowd of people into the resistance movement. But he singles out only the religious loyalists for unreserved praise, viewing their deaths as effecting a cleansing on the whole nation in the period before the end comes. The current sufferings as well as the apostasy are signs of this end. The innocent suffering of the faithful and the infamy of the apostates calls for an appropriate response from a just God. This will be the resurrection of the "many," some to everlasting life and some to everlasting shame (12:1-4). On that great day, with Michael in charge in heaven and Israel in the center of events, the wise will be glorified or resurrected in a way that transcends the current earthly conditions. This is the first reference to everlasting life in the Bible, and one of two explicit references to the resurrection itself in the Old Testament (see also Isa. 26:19).

The four visions reach their climax with Antiochus' persecution. Daniel's message is clear. Now is the time of decision for those in Israel, and the choice is an either-or. If you choose the way of least resistance, and join with an earthly, temporal kingdom, you will perish with it. God's kingdom is an everlasting kingdom. If you remain loyal to it, even if you suffer death for it, God will give you everlasting life in his kingdom.

4 The First Book of Enoch

The book of Enoch did not pass the test for admission into the canon of the Bible, even though a number of early Christians viewed it with interest and favor. Jude quoted Enoch as though it were inspired prophecy when he was writing about heretics in the Christian fellowship, people without roots or substance and thus resembling waterless clouds, fruitless trees, wild waves of the sea, and "wandering stars for whom the nether gloom of darkness has been reserved for ever" (Jude 13). Then quoting Enoch 1:9, he states: "It was of these also that Enoch in the seventh generation from Adam prophesied, saying, 'Behold, the Lord came with his holy myriads, to execute judgment on all, and to convict all the ungodly of all their deeds of ungodliness which they have committed in such an ungodly way, and of all the harsh things which ungodly sinners have spoken against him'" (Jude 14-15). Because of this quotation, the book of Jude's admittance into the Christian Bible caused some controversy. Jude finally passed the test of canonicity with rather low marks, but Enoch failed it badly, and for some good reasons. By the third and fourth centuries of the Christian era, Enoch was discredited by the Christian fathers and had passed out of circulation. It was lost to western Christianity until the nineteenth century when a copy was found in Ethiopia and translated from Ethiopic into various modern western languages, including English.

The rediscovery and translation of 1 Enoch produced a number of important links that were missing in the history of ideas during the centuries just before the Christian era. R. H. Charles has pointed out that the history of the development of Jewish thought in these important centuries could not be written without the book of Enoch.[1] Enoch dealt with a smorgasbord of subjects at a time when doctrinal thought was still very fluid in Judaism. Some of his images and ideas are bizarre and farfetched, and this explains why the book fell out of favor with later Christians. Yet there is no doubt that several of these subjects, such as the existence of demons, the coming judgment, and the person and function of the "Son of Man" in that judgment, are also important topics in the New Testament. A survey of Enoch then gives a better background perspective from which to study the New Testament as well as having historical value for doctrinal development within Judaism.

Of course, Enoch is a pseudonym for the Enoch named in Genesis 5:24. This righteous man "walked with God and was not, for God took him." Certain Jews, taking a clue from Elijah's transfiguration (cf. 2 Kings 2), concluded that this meant Enoch was also transfigured into heaven. So in chapter after chapter, Enoch is a heavenly tourist who is escorted around by one of the archangels.

In Genesis, Enoch was the great-great-grandfather of Shem, the traditional father of the Semites, as well as the great-great-grandfather of Ham and Japheth, the fathers of the African and Indo-European nations. What was his true nationality? F. C. Burkitt has said of Enoch that "no spot on the wide world is alien to him, though its center is still Jerusalem." [2] The outlook of the book is truly cosmopolitan; the sun and moon and stars, about which Enoch wrote so much, shine on both Jew and Gentile. Furthermore, the corruption of evil and the judgment that necessarily follows reaches to all men.

Actually, the book is a composite of five originally separate writings that were combined into one work by Jewish scribes. Even a casual reading shows this to be the case, because the reader moves from one block of subject matter to another in working through the book. These sections were originally written either in Hebrew or Aramaic by different authors and at different times, perhaps over a hundred years apart. R. H. Charles has argued that despite the various authors there is still a uniformity, because all the authors were either Hasidim or their successors, the Pharisees. Some later scholars like Oesterley have taken issue with Charles on the exact dating and authorship of the book.[3]

The contents of Enoch, considered approximately in the order in which they were written, are:

Chapters 1-5, Introduction.

Chapter 6-36, Vision and theodicy of Enoch.

Chapters 83-90, The dream-visions.

Chapters 72-82, Book of the heavenly luminaries.

Chapters 91-105, The Messianic kingdom.

Chapter 106-108, Fragments of the book of Noah.

Chapters 37-71, The parables or similitudes of Enoch.

Introduction, Visions, Theology (Chapters 1–36)

A short introduction, which may have been written by the final author or redactor, announces the coming judgment on the worlds (chaps. 1-5). Chapters 6-36 were written in the second century b.c., perhaps even in the pre-Maccabean period in Charles' estimation. A large part of this section is a theodicy, vindicating God's sovereignty and justice over against the evil that exists in the world.

The form of this section is a rather confused travelog in which Enoch has a series of visions. There is some confusion due in part to some textual omissions and changes. The drama begins with a dream in which Enoch is asked to intercede for the fallen angels. He writes out the petition which they make, retiring to await the answer. The angels' petition is refused. Enoch then undertakes a series of journeys through different parts of the earth, down into Sheol, and finally to the luminaries of heaven. He is guided through these journeys by the angels of light, and he includes an account of the seven archangels of God and each of their functions (chap. 20). These journeys are not made simply as curiosity tours but are meant to reassure the faithful that the heavenly world is indeed real.

The theology of this section is also strange and speculative in a number of ways. The cause of evil is traced to the rebellious and fallen angels, the "watchers," who lusted after the daughters of men. When these wicked angels intermarried with them they produced giants on the earth (cf. Gen. 6:1-4); these giants were so powerful that ordinary men could not stand up against them. These giants proceeded to destroy the rest of mankind, did violence to the other earthly creatures, and generally made the earth corrupt. Original sin, then, came through the lustful actions of the fallen angels, according to 1 Enoch. This is altogether a different theology from that of the later rabbis, the apostle Paul, and the early Christian fathers, who traced original sin to the disobedience of Adam; Enoch's speculation on the origin of evil was one reason why the book was discredited by later Christian fathers, especially Augustine in the fifth century.

The flood destroyed these giants, but their spirits continue to infest the air as demons, thus explaining every form of corruption (15:8ff.). They will continue to exercise their authority until the final judgment when they, together with wicked men, shall receive their just punishment (10:6; 16:1; 19:1). The souls of those who have died and thus are in Sheol will be separated into three groups at the judgment. Those sinners who died without being justly punished on earth are transferred from Sheol to Gehenna, or hell, where they will be punished forever (22:10-11). Those sinners who receive their just punishment while on earth will stay in Sheol forever (22:12-13). The righteous will rise with their bodies, eat of the tree of life, and live on a purified earth in a kingdom whose center is Jerusalem (25:4-6; 10:20-22). The blessedness of these righteous is pictured in a sensual way, however. They are described as each having a thousand children, and each seed that is sown will produce a thousand grains (10:17, 19). Production will keep pace with population in this Golden Age! Yet the vision does have prophetic and ethical insight. Even the Gentiles will worship God in this kingdom (10:21); the earth will be cleansed from defilement (10:22); and "truth and peace shall be together throughout all the days of the world" (11:2). This is the Messianic age, although there is no personal Messiah mentioned in this section. God himself will rule from the throne that is set upon the high earthly mountain at the time of the final judgment (25:3).

The Dream-visions (Chapters 83-90)

This apocalypse was probably written during the Maccabean period between 165-160 B.C. It consists of two dream-visions which Enoch tells to his son Methuselah. Both of these visions are distinguishable apocalyptic works on the basis of literary form and internal content. The first vision is of a cosmic catastrophe in which the heavens collapse and the earth is swallowed up in a great abyss (chaps. 83-84). After explaining the vision to his grandfather, Enoch is told to pray to the Lord that a remnant might remain on the earth.

The second vision is the "Animal Apocalypse" (chaps. 85-90). It gives a history of the world from Adam down to the last judgment and the setting up of the messianic kingdom. Taking a clue from Ezekiel 34, men are represented by animals. The patriarchs are bulls and sheep; the Gentiles are wild beasts and birds of prey ("lions, tigers, wolves, dogs, hyenas, wild boars, foxes, squirrels, swine, falcons, vultures, kites, eagles, and ravens" 89:10; cf. Ezek. 39:17); the later faithful Israelites are the sheep, with the lambs being the Hasidim who appeal in vain to the erring nation; the great horned lamb is probably Judas Maccabeus (Charles), though possibly also the later John Hyrcanus (Schürer).

Again the author is concerned with reconciling God's righteousness with the sufferings of the elect people on earth. Enoch's answer to the problem takes the form of a survey of Semitic history. He deals with the first world judgment, tracing it to the sin of the fallen angels who had intermarried with mankind. But his main concern is with the tragedies of Israel since the exile. He acknowledges that Israel has sinned, but here severe punishment has been out of proportion to her actual guilt. This is because the seventy shepherds, representing the seventy Gentile nations, into whose care God committed Israel, have overly chastised Israel (89:59). These seventy shepherds are accountable to God, and they will soon be judged for this excess punishment. When the oppression is at its worst, a righteous league will be established in Israel. This league consists of the white sheep (90:6), probably representing the Hasidim; from them will come forth the horned lamb, who will be the deliverer of Israel. The enemies of Israel, and finally all nations of the earth, will put forth every effort to destroy this hero, but in vain. While the struggle is raging, God will intervene in person, the earth will open its mouth and swallow up Israel's enemies (90:16, 18-19). Then the lustful angels, who brought woe to the earth through their sin with women, and the seventy shepherds that have oppressed Israel will be judged; both will be condemned to the abyss of fire (90:20-25). The apostate Jews will be judged next, and also condemned to Gehenna (90:26-27). Then God will set up the new Jerusalem (90:28-29), the surviving non-Jewish nations will be converted and serve Israel (90:30), the dispersed Jews will be brought back, and the righteous dead in Israel will be raised to participate in the kingdom (90:33). Then the Messiah will appear, all the righteous will be transformed into his likeness, and God will rule over them.

There is a definite theological advance in the "Animal Apocalypse" when compared to the earliest part of 1 Enoch. The concept of the next life is less sensuous. More important, the writer believes in a personal Messiah, although this Messiah has no function, for he will come after the judgment. There is no mention of him coming in David's line, as in the apocalypse of the Psalms of Solomon, which was written in the first century b.c. He will only be a human figure, coming from the bosom of the community, and will make the sheep of Israel rejoice.

The Heavenly Luminaries (Chapters 72–82)

The covenant religion of the Hebrews forbade idolatry of any kind. This marked them off from their pagan neighbors, whose worship of the sun, moon, and stars was a common part of the religion. There were times when Israelites lapsed into a worship of heavenly deities and were rebuked by the prophets (see Jer. 44 for an example). Though worship of astral deities was forbidden, the movements of the heavenly bodies was a source of continual fascination to the Israelites. 1 Enoch 72-82 reflects this interest and is an attempt to bring the laws and movements of the earth and heavenly bodies into one system. It is usually referred to as "The Book of the Courses of the Heavenly Luminaries."

This book was most likely written after the Maccabean wars had ended. The attitude of the author is more relaxed and reflective, indicating a quieter period of history. Thus, the section probably was written late in the second century B.C., when Israel had a brief respite from war and persecution.

The author's interest is a "scientific" one colored by Jewish ideas and beliefs of that time. The laws by which the sun, moon, and the stars are governed are described in detail by the angel Uriel to Enoch. The pagan signs of the zodiac have been replaced by twelve portals, three located in each major direction. The language is picturesque and mythical. The sun ascends from an eastern portal on a chariot driven by the wind, and descends into a western portal. Time is reckoned by the sun, and not by the moon. The year consists of 364 days, having eight months of 30 days, and four of 31 days. It is strange that the writer did not know from observation that the solar year had 365¼ days. Charles argues that his reckoning of the year at 364 days was partly due to his opposition to heathen systems, and partly to the fact that 364 is divisible by seven, thus amounting to exactly fifty-two weeks.[4] This opposition to the lunar year suggests that the author was a Sadducee. The Sadducees and Pharisees arose as parties in Judaism after the Maccabean wars, and the way of reckoning time, whether by the solar or lunar year, was a matter on which they differed.

The section moves along consistently until 80:1 when Enoch's tour with the angel ends. In 80:2-8 there is a complete change of ideas. Prior to this section, there was a "scientific" description wherein the movement of the heavenly bodies was fixed. Now there is an ethical section wherein man's moral actions affect natural events; perversions in nature and disorders in the heavenly bodies are traced to the sin of men.

The end of the book is also confusing. The author states the four parts of the year and names their leaders (82:13-14), but then discusses only two of the four seasons (82:15-20). Like Schubert's Eighth Symphony, this book is unfinished. The end of the book likely was lost somewhere in the transmission, perhaps through the omission of a redactor or a copyist.

This book is hardly a "bell-ringer." The author is more of a detached observer of cosmic movements than an involved participant in the drama of divine and human interaction in history.

The Messianic Kingdom (Chapters 91–105)

Both the style and spirit of this book are very different from the book of the luminaries. The author was surely not a Sadducee because be believed in a future punishment and reward. It was probably written around 100 B.C.

In its literary format this book resembles Old Testament wisdom literature such as Proverbs and Ecclesiastes. Enoch calls his sons together, and proceeds to speak to them in direct address, frequently using the term "my sons." This setting serves to introduce the main theme, which is the contrast between the sinners and the righteous. The righteous, though poor and oppressed on earth, will be vindicated and rewarded; the wicked sinners, though rich and powerful on earth, will be judged and punished. There are also two separate sections which, when put together, comprise the "Apocalypse of Weeks" (chaps. 93 and 91:12-17).

The earlier section of the book is written in the style of a debate between the sinners and the righteous. Following this, the author speaks directly and vividly in turn to each of the two groups; in spirit, and to a certain extent in style, he reflects the message of the prophets and the psalmists. Though the wicked prosper, they will be punished. There are at least nine "woe sections" that express rebuke and warning (94:6-11; 95:4-7; 96:4-8; 97:7-10; 98:9-16; 99:1-2; 99:11-16; 100:7-13; 103:5-8). The riches of the wealthy are not a sign of God's blessing, but rather a source of delusion for them: "Woe unto you, ye sinners, for your riches make you appear like the righteous, but your hearts convict you of being sinners, and this fact shall be a testimony against you for a memorial of (your) evil deeds" (96:4). Their reward will be that of future torment: "Woe to you, ye sinners, when ye have died, if ye die in the wealth of your sins . . . And now they have died in prosperity and in wealth, and have not seen tribulation or murder in their life . . . Know ye, that their souls will be made to descend into Sheol, and they shall be wretched in their great tribulation. And into darkness and chains and a burning flame where there is grievous judgment shall your spirits enter" (103:5-8). Sheol has now become Gehenna, or hell!

The righteous who have been oppressed complain about their miserable earthly situation: "We hoped to be the head and have become the tail: we have toiled laboriously and had no satisfaction in our toil; and we have become the food of the sinners and the unrighteous, and they have laid their yoke heavily upon us" (103:11). Yet they should not despair, for their present misery is a temporal and earthly experience that will be reversed in heaven: "I swear unto you, that in heaven the angels remember you for good before the glory of the Great One: and your names are written before the glory of the Great One. Be hopeful; for aforetime ye were put to shame through ill and affliction; but now ye shall shine as the lights of heaven, ye shall shine and ye shall be seen, and the portals of heaven shall be opened to you" (104:1, 2). The day of glorification for the righteous by the Great One, or the Most High (common terms for God in this book) is at hand!

The "Apocalypse of Weeks" is typical of this style of literature in giving a sweeping summary of world history in just a few verses. The first seven weeks give an account of history from Enoch's birth in the first week, through the stories of Abraham, Moses, the construction and destruction of the Temple, to the seventh week when an apostate generation will arise, to be followed by the "elect righteous of the eternal plant of righteousness" at the close of that week (93:10). The author obviously believed that he and his listeners were living in the seventh week. But there are still three weeks to follow. The messianic kingdom will be set up in the eighth week of world history. This will also be the first act of the final judgment when the wicked are given into the hands of the righteous (91:12, 13). In the ninth week, the righteous judgment shall be revealed to the whole world and the works of the godless shall be written down for destruction (91:14). In the tenth week there will be the great eternal judgment in which the Great King will execute vengeance upon the wicked angels; then the first heaven will pass away and a new heaven appear and the powers of the heavens shall give sevenfold light; this will be followed by "many weeks without number for ever, and all shall be in goodness and righteousness, and sin shall no more be mentioned for ever" (91:15-17).

The themes in the closing part of this apocalypse remind us, though still indistinctly, of the last three chapters of the book of Revelation. The apocalyptist no longer envisions a messianic age on earth, but a future for the righteous in a new heaven where they will become companions of the heavenly host. They are raised as spirits; there is no bodily resurrection affirmed here in this portion of 1 Enoch. This advance in faith and insight comes only in the Parables of Enoch, Chapters 37-71.

The Parables of Enoch (Chapters 37–71)

The theological ideas in Chapters 37-71 are the most advanced in all Jewish apocalyptic literature. This section is the latest major part of 1 Enoch, although there is considerable disagreement over the precise time it was written. 1 Enoch 37-71 is referred to as the Parables or Similitudes of Enoch; the section has three parables although there is considerable overlapping and repetition of ideas between them. Enoch is carried by a whirlwind from the earth and set down at the end of the heavens (39:3). From there, he is shown in a vision the resting place of the righteous, the place where the righteous angels and the Elect One dwells (39:4-7). He is also shown the final judgment and fate of the wicked men and angels. All this is disclosed to him while touring the heavens in the company of the angel of peace, who is not directly named. The visions are described in the first person, usually through an oracle, although occasionally a narrative form is used to describe the place or setting of the vision.

The theological themes, in typical apocalyptic fashion, range from the origin of sin to the final judgment. God is usually referred to as the "Lord of the Spirits," though quite often he is also called the "Head of Days." As "Lord of Spirits," he is ultimately Lord over both the good and wicked angels; as the "Head of Days" he will judge angels and mankind through the Son of Man.

Sin is traced back to Satan himself. The fallen angels became subject to Satan and then led those who dwelt on earth astray (54:5-6; 55:4). On judgment day, the four archangels, Michael, Gabriel, Raphael, and Phanuel, will take the fallen angels, the hosts of Azazel, and throw them into the burning abyss. Until then, sin abounds in the world. The kings and the mighty oppress the elect ones. These earthly rulers do not trust in the Lord of Spirits but in their own scepter and glory (63:7). The righteous pray to the Lord of Spirits for vengeance and the angels join in their prayers.

Suddenly, the Head of Days will appear, and with him the Messiah. They will judge all, both angels and mankind, both the righteous and the wicked. The Messiah is not of human origin, but a supernatural being; this is a startling advance over earlier ideas. Four new titles are applied to him in the Parables of Enoch, all of which are also used in the New Testament. He is twice referred to as "His Anointed" (48:10; 52:4), which in the New Testament means "the Christ"; he is also called the "Righteous One" on two occasions (38:2; 53:6; cf. Acts 3:14; 7:52 and 22:14); he is referred to as the "Elect One" 16 times (for New Testament references see Luke 9:35 and 23:35); and 15 times he is referred to as "Son of Man" (a title which Jesus used 81 times in the Synoptic Gospels, always of himself). This being stands in a unique relationship to the Lord of Spirits and Head of Days, having been chosen as Son of Man before the creation of the world and continuing as such forever (48:2-6). He is both judge and ruler. Together with the Head of Days, he will judge the mighty rulers of the world (46:1-8), as well as Azazel and his wicked hosts (55:4). Indeed, the sum of judgment has been given to the Son of Man who will establish the congregation of the elect and the holy (62:7-8). As the one in whom righteousness dwells, he will be a staff to the righteous and a light to the Gentiles (48:4). He is worthy to rule over them, for the spirit of wisdom, insight, understanding and might all dwell in him (49:3-4).

There are also new insights concerning the resurrection and the next life in the Parables of Enoch. The righteous and the elect will be raised from the earth, and clothed with garments of glory and light (51:1-2; 62:15-16). The resurrection is not simply of the spirit, as in 1 Enoch 91-105. On the other hand, it is not a materialistic notion like the Pharisaic rabbis held, who maintained that the very atoms of the earthly body would be reconstituted and raised. This is a spiritual resurrection, which approximates Paul's discussion of the nature of the resurrection body in 1 Corinthians 15. However, it is not clear from the Parables whether both the just and the unjust will be raised. The resurrection of both is implied in 51:1, 2, but 61:5 implies that only the righteous will be raised. Perhaps this lack of precision should be viewed in the context of the variety of Jewish doctrines of the resurrection. Of course, the Sadducees believed in no resurrection at all. But even among those Jews who believed in a resurrection, as did the Pharisees, there was a variety of differing views in late Judaism. By way of summary, Charles has indicated three different doctrines:

1) all Israelites will arise: Daniel 12:2, 1 Enoch 1-36 (except 22:13); 37-71, and 83-90; 2 Maccabees 7:9 et al; 2 Baruch 50:1-51:6;

2) all righteous Israelites will arise: Isa. 25:8 and 26:19; 1

Enoch 91:105; the Psalms of Solomon; and Josephus' *Antiquities* 18. 1:3; this was also the accepted Talmudic view;

3) all mankind will arise: 2 Esdras 7:32, 37; and the Testament of the Twelve Patriarchs in Benjamin 10:6-8.[5]

The reader who has carefully read this chapter, and in particular this last section on 1 Enoch 37-71, cannot overlook the similarities between Jewish and Christian doctrines on the Messiah and the last things. Again and again, Christians need to be reminded that the roots of their faith are in Judaism. The problem then, becomes one of defining the relationship between Judaism and Christianity more clearly, trying to determine what has been inherited from Judaism and how it has been reshaped by the dynamic new faith. This gets a very specific focus when the question is asked: What is the relationship between the Son of Man in 1 Enoch 37-71 and the Son of Man sayings in the Synoptic Gospels? Interpreting these sayings remains one of the most difficult of all tasks in New Testament studies.

Since the rediscovery of 1 Enoch in Western Christianity, scholars had generally interpreted the Synoptic Son of Man sayings against the background of Daniel 7 and 1 Enoch 37-71. They assumed that these chapters were written in the first century B.C. We can no longer be sure about this assumption since the discovery of the Dead Sea scrolls at Qumran a generation ago. The discoveries in the wilderness community turned up texts or commentaries on every Old Testament book except Esther, and also texts of every part of 1 Enoch—except chapters 37-71! This raised the important question whether these chapters had even been written at the time of Jesus' ministry, and whether or not the Son of Man sayings in the Parables of Enoch even predate the Gospel sayings themselves. Admittedly, this is an argument from silence which is not very convincing. However, the failure to find any evidence of the Parables of Enoch at Qumran, this most apocalyptic of all Jewish sects, means that we can no longer assume direct dependence of the Gospel sayings upon 1 Enoch 37-71. Scholars are now dating these chapters anywhere from the first century B.C. to the early part of the second century A.D., with the first century A.D. as the most frequent suggestion.

The previous paragraph may seem to some readers to be an unnecessary little side trip into the underbrush, even into the jungle, of biblical and historical studies. It is only an example of clearing a small portion of the path that leads to a better understanding of the Judaeo-Christian heritage. The Christian is urged to add knowledge to his faith, always aware that the Son of Man is one who fits no easy formula. While we can no longer assume a direct relationship between the Son of Man in 1 Enoch 37-71 and the Son of Man in the Synoptic Gospels, they share a crucial core idea. The Son of Man will judge justly and will rule in righteousness. Here too, then, is a common hope in the ultimate triumph of God's kingdom in which the righteous and the elect, the saints of God, will have a glorious part.

5 An Apocalyptic Sect: The Qumran Community

Palestine is a land of infinite variety. Jerusalem and Qumran are less than 20 miles apart, yet they are different worlds. Jerusalem, located in the highlands of Judea, is almost 2600 feet above sea level; consequently, it has a temperate climate with generally mild days, even in midsummer. By contrast, temperatures down at Qumran near the Dead Sea are tropical. Located about 1200 feet below sea level, summertime temperatures are almost unbearably hot, often reaching 100° and sometimes going up to 120°. Jerusalem receives a considerable amount of precipitation during the rainy season; Qumran, on the eastern side of the highland, receives much less. Except for the spring of Ain Feshqa, immediately to the south, nothing grows in the immediate area of Qumran. No fish or marine life can exist in the Dead Sea.

The excavated ruins of the Qumran community stand on a plateau of white marl. Looking to the east, one sees the Dead Sea less than a mile away and beyond that the hills of Jordan. To the west are the steep, rugged hills that lead up into the wilderness region between the Dead Sea and the city of Jerusalem. Although the scenery in the area is stunning, the ruins themselves are not particularly impressive. They reveal what was a rectangular structure, about 100 by 200 feet, consisting of a dining hall, a library, a bakery, and a potter's kiln. There was also an elaborate system of cisterns to catch and hold water which drained down the long watercourse, or wadi, stretching from just east of Jerusalem down to the north corner of the Dead Sea. On a nearby hillside is a cemetery, containing about a thousand graves. Looking across a deep ravine, one sees a large, artificial cave in the rugged hillside. This is Cave 4, where thousands of fragments of parchments have been discovered, including fragments from every Old Testament book except Esther. About a mile to the north is Cave 1, which was accidentally discovered by a Bedouin shepherd boy in 1947.

It was this discovery that set in motion the later archaeological work under the direction of Father Roland de Vaux. This resulted in fabulous manuscript discoveries, turning up scrolls which exceeded the age of previously known Old Testament manuscripts by a thousand years. It also brought to light a body of literature produced by the Qumran community, as well as the unearthing of the remains of the community's main structure that had been burned by the invading Roman armies in 68 A.D. Exploration revealed numerous caves, eleven of which contained scrolls or fragments of scrolls. These caves were explored and excavated between 1949 and 1961. Pottery, pieces of cloth, and coins, all dating from the first and second centuries B.C. and the first century A.D. were also found. The process of preserving and studying the manuscripts continues. They are now preserved and on display in the impressive museum, the Shrine of the Book in Jerusalem, which was especially built to house these priceless finds.

Several documents among the Qumran literature are of particular importance for understanding the community. The general laws of everyday life as well as regulations for admission to the community were contained in a seven-foot leather scroll known as the Manual of Discipline; two columns bearing the title, "Rule of the Congregation," were attached to the beginning of the Manual. A large scroll contains a collection of Thanksgiving Hymns; in spirit these resemble the Psalms of the Old Testament and were probably written by the Teacher, the founder of the community. The commentaries on Old Testament books, particularly those on Habakkuk and Isaiah, are especially significant in that they reveal how the Qumran people interpreted their Scriptures. A battle plan for the final war between Israel and her enemies is laid out in the scroll, "The War of the Sons of Light with the Sons of Darkness." A document that was known by scholars before the discoveries at Qumran, having been first found in a storeroom of a Cairo synagogue in 1910, is the Damascus Document. It received this name because it laid down rules to govern a Jewish group living in the "camps" of the land of "Damascus." After the Six-Day War of 1967, Jews found a large scroll in Old Jerusalem, which Professor Yigael Yadin has named the Temple Scroll. It is believed that the scroll may have come from Cave 11. Written in the first person, the scroll gives instructions for building the temple according to the description of the tabernacle in Exodus 35-38.

Life in the Qumran Community

The people who left mild and balmy Jerusalem and migrated to the hot and barren region near the Dead Sea were driven by powerful convictions. The rulers in Jerusalem and the men who founded Qumran in the second century B.C. lived in different

religious worlds. The legal high priesthood ended with the depo-
sition of Onias III in 175 B.C. The roots of Qumran probably
reach back to this time and the Maccabean wars that followed.
The later Maccabeans, also known as the Hasmoneans, became
corrupt within a generation. There was conflict between the
leaders in power and the enthusiasts for the Law. From the
Qumran documents, we learn that the "Wicked Priest" persecuted the "Teacher of Righteousness." There are various theories
concerning the identity of these figures. Whether the Teacher
was Onias II or whether he lived later in the century and was
the figure persecuted by the Hasmonean priest Jonathan (1 Macc.
10:18-20), is difficult to establish. At any rate, the Teacher and
his followers were stern spokesmen for the Law. They accused
the leadership in Israel of compromise, of "serving God with a
double heart." The Jerusalem leaders were "false prophets, en-
ticed by error," who spoke with "foreign tongues." Israel had
taken a dark and dangerous turn under such leadership.

In this situation the devout "remained like blind men groping
their way, until at last God took note of their deeds, that they
were seeking him sincerely, and he raised up for them one (the
Teacher) who would teach the Law correctly, to guide them in
the way of his heart . . ." (The Damascus Document). This
Teacher, himself necessarily a priest, then led his followers forth
from Jerusalem in an exodus-like march to the barren regions
of the Dead Sea. Taking a clue from Isaiah 40:3, there in the
"wilderness" they would "prepare the way of the Lord" through
the devoted study of the Law. Though the nation as a whole
was apostate, God had raised up a righteous "remnant," his
"elect ones." They had gone into the wilderness to save Israel
by establishing the New Covenant that Jeremiah had promised
(Jer. 31:31-34). They regarded themselves as the true Israel living

in the last days of history. Consequently, every impurity, every trace of darkness, was to be excluded from this holy community.

This background explains the beliefs and practices of the strange community at Qumran. They were a sect, dissenters who intentionally separated themselves from the mainstream of Israel's life for religious reasons. Furthermore, they were an apocalyptic sect, fully convinced that the ungodliness and darkness that now prevailed was a sign of the imminent end of the present age. And so this apocalyptic sect at Qumran, deeply conscious of the priestly heritage from the past, but keenly anticipating God's judgment in the near future, set up a priestly dominated, self-enclosed, and apocalyptically-minded community in the desert wastes near the Dead Sea. There is no modern parallel to this community. It combined pre-Vatican II Roman Catholic priestly consciousness and power, high church Anglican ritualism, Amish asceticism, Hutterite communalism, Orthodox Jewish legalism, Pentecostal zeal and fervor, and Jehovah's Witness apocalypticism in its life and worship. With the exception of a few years following an earthquake in 31 B.C., this group lived at Qumran from about 135 B.C. to 68 A.D.

The authority in this rigid community was committed to the priests, commonly referred to as either the "sons of Zadok" or the "sons of Aaron." The exact details of the organization are difficult to determine, because there are differences between the Damascus Document and the Manual of Discipline and the War Scroll on the subject. These writings probably date from different periods and reflect some changes in the community's structure. However, absolute loyalty to one's superiors was always required. One priest, who had to be between 30 and 50 years old, was in charge of the community. There was an examiner, also of the same age, who instructed the members in the works of God and supervised a wide range of their activities. There was a body of presbyters, 15 in number, that was responsible for the faith and life of the community. "In the deliberative council of the community there shall be twelve laymen and three priests schooled to perfection in all that has been revealed of the entire Law" (The Manual of Discipline). Admission membership, which was limited to male Israelite adults, was a two-year process that involved careful instruction and four thorough examinations during that period. Outsiders seeking membership were carefully screened to keep out the wicked, the weak, and the doubtful. Those with mental and physical handicaps were automatically excluded because they would defile the community. Members owned no personal property, because everything was put into a common fund.

Ritual was very important in such an ordered community. Sacred baths, or washings, were common at Qumran. The initiate took a first bath, following his oath. This seems similar to baptism, yet it was not identical with it because sacred baths were taken periodically by all members as a symbol of purity. The Qumran members seem to have spent a lot of time taking baths, which is perhaps not surprising in that hot, forbidding climate! Every communal meal had a certain religious meaning, with a priest saying grace before and after the meal. Occasionally, more formal ritual banquets were held in anticipation of the messianic banquet that would take place when God's kingdom was finally victorious over the forces of Belial, the devil (cf. Luke 22:15-18). The covenant was renewed annually in an impressive service that involved the whole community, priests, Levites, and lay members (cf. Josh. 24 and Deut. 25). The priests recalled the mighty acts and promises of God; the Levites made antiphonal response, reciting the curse that rested on the evil men of Belial. Then the whole community, robed in white, passed "into the covenant" in a ceremony that probably involved a sacred bath.

While salvation was by God's grace—some portions of the Thanksgiving Hymns are very evangelical—only those who kept the Law according to the interpretation of the community were saved. If the community was to remain free of darkness, it had to know God's Law and interpret it in accordance with the views of the Teacher of Righteousness. Therefore, every third night was to be spent studying the scriptures together. "The Many shall keep watch together a third of the nights of all the year, reading the book and searching for justice, and worshiping together" (The Manual of Discipline). Study groups consisted of a minimum of ten members, and a priest had to be present at each session. Careful attention was given to legal elements in the Old Testament, especially to those rules governing the Sabbath. The Damascus Document lists 27 rules defining proper Sabbath observance. A rigid system of rules governed the members' lives, with severe penalties for disobedience. A member who consciously lied about his wealth would be fined one-fourth of his food ration. Speaking in anger against one of the registered priests would mean isolation from the community for a year; spitting during a public meeting, falling asleep during a public meeting, or loud, raucous laughter would each cost a man 30 days isolation. Grumbling against the institution of the community would result in banishment for life.

All of this priestly structure, ritualism, and legalism was regarded as necessary to beat out the evil and darkness in sinful human nature and to make a man a true "son of light." This pure community would be the holy remnant through which God would act to gather a New Israel and annihilate the forces of Belial at the end of the age.

The Final War

The people of Qumran believed that the present evil age would come to an end with a great final battle. Before that would take place, God would raise up two Messiahs, the one a priestly and the second a lay Messiah. The priestly Messiah, who was expected to come from the house of Zadok and presumably then from the ranks of Qumran, would be a prophet who would fulfill the promise of Deuteronomy 18:18. The lay Messiah, believed to be coming from the house of David, would be a military man fulfilling the promise of Numbers 24:15-17. Through these men the traditional leadership of Israel would be restored in a New Israel; then the fallen booth of David would be raised up once again (cf. Amos 9:11). The priest and prince would stand shoulder to shoulder in governing Israel, as Solomon and Zadok had done centuries before. In Qumran, however, as also in the apocryphal writing of the Testament of the Twelve Patriarchs, the anointed priest was expected to be a much more important figure than the anointed prince.

But while Israel would be restored, there was no hope for the Gentile world. These nations were under the control of Belial, and the only solution to this evil situation was to be a future war in which they would be destroyed. This theme is expressed in The War of the Sons of Light and the Sons of Darkness, ordinarily referred to as the War Scroll.

The scroll lists certain enemies of Israel from Old Testament times, including the Edomites, Moabites, Ammonites, and Philistines. The Kittim of Assyria and the Kittim of Egypt are also named; the Kittim probably referred to the Romans, although some scholars have thought it referred to the Macedonian Greeks. There is also a reference to Gog, a northern power whose destruction was foretold in Ezekiel 38-39. These forces collectively are called the Sons of Darkness.

The Sons of Light were expected to return from their exile to pitch camp in the desert of Jerusalem. They would be joined by other Israelites who would come *from* Jerusalem to the camp. From this camp the Sons of Light would wage war upon the Sons of Darkness.

The war as described here is really a crusade, with God as both Warrior and Judge in the conflict. It is a war involving angels as well as men. The archangel Michael (cf. Dan. 12:1), together with Gabriel, Sariel, and Raphael (cf. 1 Enoch 20, 40) were depicted as leading the armies of Israel, while the hosts of Belial support the enemy. The details concerning the camp and the conduct of the war itself reflect the concept of the Holy War, particularly as it was fought in Israel before the time of King David. The religious slogans on the trumpets, banners, and blades of the battle-darts, the prayers to be spoken by the priests before and after each battle, the number and exact battle order of the 6000 cavalry and 28,000 combat troops, the number of battle charges and countercharges, and even the number of battle-darts to be hurled are all prescribed in the War Scroll.

The camp itself is a holy place and must be kept ceremonially clean and undefiled. No women or children, or lame or blind or crippled people may enter to defile it. Even the latrines must be about 3000 feet from the camp. The soldiers on the front line must be 40 to 50 years old so that their ages correspond to those of the Old Testament priests. The war is described as lasting 40 years, but the fighting will not be continuous because every seventh year will be a sabbatical year. The result will be the total destruction of the Sons of Darkness; the writer envisions the end of the war as the time "when the sons of Japheth fall never to rise, and when the Kittim are cut off without survivor." Conversely, it will be the day when "the rule of Michael will be exalted among the angels, and the dominion of Israel among all flesh."

There has been a variety of interpretations of the War Scroll since its discovery a generation ago. Did the writer foresee an actual final battle in history or was he describing a spiritual battle? In trying to answer this question, we should remember that the people at Qumran looked at all of reality in a dualistic way. God and Belial, good and evil, light and darkness were forces that struggled for control of the events going on around them. According to the Manual of Discipline, the spirits of good and evil struggle in the heart of men. The forces of good and evil, represented by the Teacher of Righteousness and the Wicked Priest, also struggled for control in Israel. The forces of light and darkness again struggle in the war between Israel and Gentile nations. Finally, there is a cosmic struggle between the heavenly hosts led by the Lord and those hosts of evil led by Belial. These historical and cosmic elements of the conflict are clearly present in the War Scroll, and it would appear that the unknown writer of this document envisioned a war in the not too distant future when Israel would triumph over all her enemies. His trouble was that he, too, closely identified the interests of his own sect and that of Israel with the Lord's plan. The end did come for Qumran, but the result was very different from the writer's expectations. In A.D. 68 the Roman armies of Vespasian burned the buildings of the community, and its members either fled or were captured or killed. Yet this tragic end of the devout men of Qumran did not mean the destruction of God's plans, for he is greater than any religious community or nation of men.

The War Scroll and the book of Revelation deal with common themes such as the conflict between good and evil, but there are striking differences when the two are more carefully compared.

No one personality is dominant in the War Scroll as Jesus Christ is in Revelation. The Teacher of Righteousness, for example, is not mentioned in the War Scroll and a crusade mentality pervades: God is on our side and his will is done by destroying the enemy. The words of a World War II song, "Praise the Lord and pass the ammunition," glibly but fairly accurately summarize this self-righteous view. In Revelation, the conflict between good and evil is no less real, but God uses evil forces to purge and cleanse his people, and thus the call to repentance and faith and patient endurance is repeated again and again throughout the book. Finally, there is no thought in the War Scroll of saving any of the Gentiles; the Sons of Darkness will be totally annihilated. By contrast, the new Jerusalem that comes down from God will bring God's light by which the nations will walk, and the leaves of the tree of life will be for the healing of the nations (Rev. 21:24 and 22:1-2).

Qumran and Christianity

The study of the Dead Sea Scrolls raises many questions, but the most controversial is the influence, if any, of the Qumran community on Christianity and the early church. By the middle 1950s the controversy was getting considerable attention through published books and articles.[1] Since the Qumran community and the Dead Sea Scrolls existed prior to the Christian church and the New Testament, the issue is whether or not Christianity originated at Qumran and drew its main teachings from that community.

No one can deny that there are some striking similarities between Qumran and the early church. Members of both communities believe in a living God who had revealed himself to Israel through the Law and the prophets and would judge the world at the end of history. Both communities traced their origins to a central personality who had been persecuted by wicked men. Both communities regarded themselves as a fellowship of believers that used a washing with water in admitting new members, gathered for fellowship meals that had a sacramental character, and studied the Hebrew Scriptures diligently to discover God's will for them in the present. Yet similarities by themselves do not prove dependence, and the assertions by some that Christianity originated at Qumran need to be carefully tested.

This testing might begin with John the Baptist, for if there is a link between the two movements it is he. John began his ministry in the wilderness of Judea, just a few miles from Qumran. He preached a coming judgment for which the people must get ready or else face the fire. He baptized those who repented. He himself practiced a stern life-style similar to the holy poverty of the Qumranians. Qumran was an Essene community, or at least an Essene-like one. We know from Josephus that the Essenes did not marry, but that they adopted young children, and raised them to observe their ways (Josephus, *Wars of the Jews,* vii. 2). We also know that John was born to very old and devout parents. It is entirely possible, then, that John was adopted and raised by the men at Qumran after the death of his parents, and from them he acquired his stern manners and message.[2]

This interesting possibility needs to be tested to see how well it stands up under examination, using the Gospels and the Dead Sea Scrolls as sources. There are at least four areas where John and the Qumranians may be compared: the wilderness tradition; their ascetic life-style; the interpretation of Isaiah 40:3; and John's baptism and the washings at Qumran.

According to Luke 1:80, the child John was in the wilderness until the time of his public appearance to Israel; this is evidently the wilderness area west of the Dead Sea. In addition, the Fourth

Gospel mentions John preaching at Bethany beyond the Jordan, and at Aenon, near Salim (John 1:28; 3:23); these were cities located on main trading routes of the time and within a day's journey of Qumran. The people who withdrew from Israel, and settled in the wilderness at Qumran believed that they were reliving the exodus experience. In separating from the apostate in Jerusalem, they had entered into a new covenant experience in the wilderness. The wilderness was for both John and Qumran a place of retreat and renewal.

John lived an ascetic manner of life (Mark 1:6). To the modern worshiper, the Advent texts on John the Baptist probably remind him of some Tarzan-like figure, but actually John's dress was the mark of an ascetic prophet. His food was the simplest of nature foods, and his whole style of life was geared to an inner change of heart that prepared him for the imminent judgment day. The men at Qumran dressed in white, symbolizing purity of life. The community rules concerning food and sleep were strict—though not as exact as those of the Pharisees—and were meant to prepare them for the coming day of the Lord.

Both John and the Dead Sea Scrolls put a heavy emphasis on Isaiah 40:3: "A voice cries, 'In the wilderness prepare the way of the Lord, make straight in the desert a highway for our God.' " All four Gospels refer to this verse in the opening lines of their John the Baptist pericopes. John is preparing the way of the Lord in the wilderness by preaching to the multitudes. But Qumran interpreted this text very differently: "The reference (in Isa. 40:3) is to the study of the Law which God commanded through Moses . . ." (The Manual of Discipline). They were preparing the way by an introverted study of the Law led by their elders. This was an exclusive understanding of Isaiah 40:3; John's was an inclusive application.

Finally, John preached a baptism of repentance for *all* people.

The distinguishing feature of his mission was that all who repented were baptized with a proselyte baptism that was ordinarily required only of Gentiles who converted to Judaism. There is no evidence that Qumran immediately baptized people who were repentant. On the contrary, the Manual of Discipline suggests that a convert was permitted to take the first oath and admitted to the first bath only after a long probationary period, and then only after the community had voted to accept him. John's baptism was an act, a public state of repentance; the first bath at Qumran was part of a process that finally admitted one into a formal state of purity. The baptism that John administered had quite a different character from the washings at Qumran.

The evidence shows that John was not a sectarian. As the Synoptic Gospels state when referring to him as Elijah, he was a prophet who stood in the main stream of Judaism. He may well have visited Qumran, or even been raised there. But there is a marked difference in his mentality and in his mission methods that suggest he had broken completely with their sectarian ways, if indeed he ever embraced them.

These differences become even more striking when Qumran and Jesus are compared. For the sake of brevity, only a few important differences are mentioned here.[3] The citizens of Qumran were even more rigid on the observance of the Law and on the details regarding Sabbath than the Pharisees, with whom Jesus differed so sharply. Qumran had no mission to the Gentiles, but Jesus on several occasions ministered to them, including the despised Samaritans. The Manual of Discipline required the members to hate all sons of darkness; Jesus said, "Love your enemies and pray for those who persecute you" (Matt. 5:43; see also Luke 6:27-28, 35; 23:34). The War Scroll mapped out, in great detail, the religious war in which the sons of darkness would be destroyed; Jesus renounced armed might and warned, "All who take the sword will perish by the sword" (Matt. 26:52; see Luke 22:38). The Qumran community had a body of secret teachings, especially on the names of angels, that it gave only to its own initiates. In contrast, when questioned by the high priest, Jesus declared that he had spoken only to the world, in synagogues and in the temple, and had said nothing secretly (John 18:20). Finally, Qumran was expecting two Messiahs, a priestly figure from the house of Aaron who would stand above the political figure from the house of David. Jesus made no mention of a Messiah from Aaron. Furthermore, he was also very careful how he used the title Christ (= Messiah) because of popular misconceptions, preferring to use the term Son of Man when speaking of his messianic role.

There is no mention in the Gospels that Jesus ever visited Qumran, or that any of them visited him. However, it is not hard to imagine such an occurrence. Like the Pharisees, and even John's disciples, they would have raised questions about his freedom (see Mark 3:18-22). Jesus' reply was a warning against putting the new wine of the Gospel into the old wineskins of Judaism. This is the fundamental difference between Jesus and Qumran. The new wine of the Gospel was too powerful and liberating to be contained in the old wineskins, even Qumran wineskins.

6 Mark 13: The Little Apocalypse

During my seminary days, I met an old gentleman who warned me, "Look out for those seminary professors!" With this warning, he referred to Jesus' statement that "This generation shall not pass away until all these things be accomplished." From this he concluded that Jesus and the church built on him were also in error. So look out for the seminary professors!

The old gentleman had raised a difficult question. The delay of the *parousia* (Greek for "presence" and "coming") was a problem for the early church. It became a pressing problem again for European Christians with the publication of David Strauss' *Life of Jesus* in 1835.[1] Mark 13 and its parallels in Matthew 24 and Luke 21 were especially heavy artillery for Strauss' assault on Christianity. The issues in the discussion, with particular regard for Mark 13, were most clearly summarized in the "Little Apocalypse" theory set forth by Timothy Colani in 1864.

The "Little Apocalypse" Theory

Like a number of scholars before him, Colani wanted no connection between Jewish Messianic ideas and Jesus. Rather than regarding Jesus as a Messiah coming in judgment from heaven, he viewed him as a prophetic preacher of the kingdom of God. This kingdom of simple righteousness, that Jesus preached, would come gradually, like an organic development, rather than suddenly through an apocalyptic catastrophe. Thus the statements about the coming of Christ in glory should be eliminated from the Gospel texts, either by interpreting them in a figurative way or regarding them as unauthentic. Given this mind set, Colani's treatment of Mark 13 was predictable. Instead of a precise reply to the disciples' question concerning the time of the temple's destruction, Jesus gave a long discourse ending with the words, "But of that day or that hour no one knows, not even the angels in heaven, nor the Son, but only the Father" (13:32). But, according to Colani, the discourse was not Jesus' doing. In response to the disciples' question, "When will it be?" he had simply answered, "I don't know." The section between Mark 13:5-31 was an insertion into the text by Jewish Christians, according to Colani. It was written by Jewish Christians about A.D. 68 at a time of severe persecution; in fact, it was this persecution which forced them to leave Judea and Jerusalem and flee to Pella in the region east of the Jordan. The discourse is full of Jewish apocalyptic elements, with a few Christian ingredients. This "Little Apocalypse" lies like a fallen boulder interrupting the path and progression of the Gospel of Mark. Luke and Matthew, who later used Mark as one of their sources, incorporated the apocalypse, with some modifications, into their own Gospel accounts. This is Colani's explanation for the origin of the chapter. Consistent with his presuppositions, he chose Jesus and abandoned the discourse.

Theologians, continuing the study after Colani, produced a great body of literature on the subject. Colani had regarded Mark 13:5-31 as a single document. Scholars after him made a careful analysis, section by section, verse by verse, and even phrase by phrase, in order to determine which were authentic sayings of Jesus and which were later additions. The conclusions of their labors were varied and sometimes contradictory. However, in general, four main current viewpoints have emerged. Bultmann's view is largely a continuation of the "Little Apocalypse" theory, for he regards the chapter as a Jewish apocalypse with a few Christian additions.[2] On the other hand, Beasley-Murray defends the whole chapter as an authentic speech of the historical Jesus.[3] A Swedish scholar argues that Old Testament prophetic material, along with traditions from Jesus, were interpreted in close relationship to the church's experience; thus Mark 13 became a "prophetic tract" on the last things for the early church.[4] A fourth position attributes the apocalyptic teaching of Jesus, as preserved by the early church, to the risen Christ, who gave special instruction to the disciples following the resurrection; Mark 13, together with Acts 1:6-12 and 1 Thessalonians 4:13ff., are traditions preserved from this instruction.[5]

An exegesis of Mark 13, which aims to "lead out" the meaning of the text and reach conclusions based on the investigation, will be made in the following pages. Such a study must first consider briefly the historical situation and purpose of the Gospel of Mark, as well as the literary context of Mark 13 within his Gospel.

The Historical Situation

The Gospel of Mark was written for Christians living in troubled times. It was a time of wars and rumors of wars (cf. Mark 13:7). Earlier, Christians had suffered at the hands of Jewish councils; now they were called to face sufferings, for the sake of Jesus, before Roman authorities (13:9). During Nero's persecution, in which Christians were made the scapegoats for the great fire which burned half of Rome in A.D. 64, many of the faithful were martyred, among them Peter and Paul. But this was not yet the end, only the beginning of the final woes (13:8, 9-13).

Palestine was becoming increasingly restless and explosive with a rising fever of political Messianic emotions (13:5, 6, 21, 22). A combination of corrupt, oppressive Roman officials in Palestine and fiery, super-nationalistic zealot feeling was the mix that ignited the conflict. The seven year war, which started in Caesarea by the sea in A.D. 66 and ended with the capture of Masada in A.D. 73, was disastrous for Palestine Jews and also proved to be the great divide between Jews and early Christians. Jerusalem and the temple were destroyed in A.D. 70 with enormous suffering and loss of life. The Jewish historian Josephus has left the most complete record of the events of these tragic years in his *Wars of the Jews*. Though a very thorough recorder, he was nevertheless an opportunist who was really on the third side of the conflict—his own! He had saved his life by going over to the Roman side in the earlier Galilean part of the war. Consequently, his writings should be taken with a grain of salt, particularly where they involve his own interpretations. For example, Josephus claimed that the Roman general Titus gave orders that the temple be spared *(Wars, VI. 4. 3.)*. On the other hand, another source, probably from Tacitus, states that Titus ordered the destruction of the temple.[6] Which source should be believed? Since the temple was the center for both Jewish religious and national life, both a national cathedral and a parliament building, especially for the militant Zealots, it is more likely that Titus ordered its destruction than its preservation. At any rate, its ruin removed the visible center of Yahweh's presence and was a disaster for all Jews. Many wept when they heard the news, as at the death of a loved one.

Jewish theology did not escape the shock waves of this disaster. The writer of the apocalyptic book of 2 Esdras is an example of the post-temple Jewish bewilderment and questioning. After wrestling with the question of God's justice in the face of such tragedy, he sees the age as "hastening swiftly to its end" (4:26), and then asks about the new age that will soon come when the predetermined number of the righteous will be completed (4:33-43). The long term effect within Judaism was the triumph of rabbinic theology. Prior to A.D. 70, there had been many theological parties and much diversity within Judaism; after that date, the creativity and diversity dried up and the arteries hardened into the prevailing form of rabbinic Judaism. The apocalyptic tradition, which had its roots in Judaism, turned out to be one of the victims of that development.

Even more tragic was the permanent split between Judaism and Christianity. In spite of tensions and troubles between Orthodox Jews and early Christian Jews, there had been a continuity between the two religions for a whole generation in Jerusalem. James, the respected and conservative leader of the church in Jerusalem, continued to worship in the temple until his death in A.D. 62. Even Paul maintained his ties with Judaism and went to the temple to make a vow (Acts 21:17-26). This continuity ended with the Jewish-Roman war and the destruction of Jerusalem. Christians regarded the destruction of the city and temple as a judgment upon the Jews for their rejection of the Messiah. On the other hand, the surviving Jews viewed the Jewish Christians as those who had forsaken the law and the religion of their fathers to embrace a new religion. The trunk was more and more separated from its root, and hostility and controversy became the norm in Jewish-Christian relations.

The Literary Context

Though he was a Christian Jew, Mark wrote his Gospel for Gentiles, especially for the Romans. A "Gospel" was a unique literary form in the ancient world. For each evangelist, his work is an account of the progress of Jesus to the cross. Mark's theme, announced in 1:14-15, focuses on Jesus, who begins his ministry preaching in Galilee. Galilee is the locale of Jesus' greatest popular success and appeal. Anointed with the Holy Spirit and with sonship at his baptism, Jesus goes throughout the region doing good and healing by God's power. After Jesus' choice of the twelve disciples, the "new Israel," the reader follows the "rising action" of Jesus' ministry in Galilee and the region beyond Galilee (1:14–8:26). With Peter's confession that Jesus is the Messiah, or Christ (8:27-30), the "plot" of his future suffering and death begins to unfold in the journey to Jerusalem (8:31–10:52). Three predictions (8:31; 9:31; 10:32-34), sounding like the repeated tolling of a bell, serve the literary function of holding together the journey narrative that takes Jesus and the disciples to Jerusalem.

In contrast to Galilee, the homeland of faith, Jerusalem is the place of danger and death. The last week of Jesus' life begins with the Palm Sunday entry (11:1-11). With Jerusalem now as the scene of action, and controversy as the dominant theme, the drama builds up to the climax of Jesus' arrest, trials, and crucifixion. At the climactic moment of Jesus' death, the curtain of the Jewish temple was torn in two, and mighty Rome, in the person of the centurion, confesses that this crucified man was the Son of God (15:38, 39; cf. the title in 1:1).

The careful reader of Mark's Gospel will observe that the writer has skillfully developed his theme within the literary framework of a "Gospel," as defined above. Furthermore, the reader will note that Jesus' entry into Jerusalem leads him to the temple, which he proceeds to cleanse (11:15-19). This is not the action of a religious reformer, but a symbolic action in the court of the Gentiles which is a curtain raiser to the time when the Gentiles will come to the eschatological temple (see Ezek. 40–48). The cleansing of the temple is sandwiched in between the cursing of the fig tree, which symbolizes unfruitful Israel that has rejected the Messiah (11:12-14), and Jesus' interpretation of the meaning of this action (11:20-25). Five controversy stories with the religious leaders follow these significant actions: 1) Jesus' assertion of authority (11:27-33); 2) Paying taxes to Caesar (12:13-17); 3) The question concerning the resurrection (12:18-27); 4) The great commandment of love (12:28-34); and 5) The decisive issue concerning David's son (12:35-37). Like beads carefully arranged on a string, Mark, the evangelist-redactor, has effectively presented Jesus' vigorous comments on several burning issues of the time. "Although they were given form by the early church, we undoubtedly come closer to the historical Jesus in these five controversy stories than in any other narratives of the synoptic tradition." [7]

The Jerusalem setting, with the particulars of the cleansing of the temple, the fig tree pronouncement, and the controversy stories, furnishes the literary context for Mark 13. Furthermore, Jesus' prediction of the temple's destruction (13:2) is used as the charge against him in the trial before Caiaphas (14:58) and at his crucifixion (15:29). Against Colani and others who have followed his interpretation, the evidence shows that Mark 13 is not an erratic boulder interrupting the progression of the Gospel content. On the contrary, with regard to both structure and theme, the chapter has an integral role in the Gospel's progression and content.

With this survey of its context, we turn to an interpretation of

Mark 13, discussing the units of the chapter in an ascending
order.

Interpretation of Mark 13

Mark 1:1-4: The setting

Jesus left the temple for the last time. He was abandoning the
place which he had earlier cleansed, and the scene of his various
controversies with the leaders. His departure had the signs of a
definite schism with the established Jerusalem religion. One of
the disciples, struck by the size and grandeur of the temple,
expressed his feelings of wonder and awe. And well might this
Galilean country boy be overwhelmed, for it was one of the
most beautiful structures in the world. Herod the Great, in
order to improve his standing with the Jews, had begun the
rebuilding of the temple in the eighteenth year of his reign
(40-4 B.C.). During the renovation, the size of the temple mount
was doubled by building gigantic supporting walls and filling
in the intervening area. The sanctuary itself, built of white
stone, was raised forty cubits and broadened thirty cubits and its
facade was renewed; its gates and many of its decorations were
plated with gold. The building process continued for many
years; John 2:20 has a reference to the building going on for
forty-six years. Undoubtedly work was still being done at the
time of Jesus' ministry, because the finishing touches were completed only a few years before its destruction in A.D. 70.

Unimpressed by the material grandeur of the temple, Jesus
soberly predicted its destruction. Some commentators have questioned whether Jesus actually made such a prediction. But centuries before, Israelite prophets had predicted the destruction of
Solomon's temple (Micah 3:12; Jer. 7:14; 26:6), which had been

fulfilled in 586 B.C. And even Jewish seers after Jesus were making similar predictions concerning Herod's temple (2 Enoch 90:28; Josephus, *Wars,* VI. 5. 3.). This is a genuine prophecy of Jesus, not a creation of the early church. In fact, its genuineness is even more attested because the temple was not literally "thrown down" in A.D. 70, but burned by the Romans. Matthew, writing after A.D. 70, has even retained Mark's precise wording (Matt. 24:2).

Jesus went to the Mount of Olives, "opposite the temple" (Mark 13:3). This height, east of Mt. Zion and Jerusalem, is in fact higher than the mountain on which the temple stood. Jesus took a clue from Zechariah 14:4 concerning the day of the Lord's coming: "On that day his feet shall stand on the Mount of Olives which lies before Jerusalem on the east." For Mark, the Mount of Olives is the eschatological counter-mountain. From this place, according to Mark and Matthew, Jesus appropriately gave his prophetic discourse.

The discourse was prompted by a private question from the disciples. Mark lists them by name: Peter, James, John, and Andrew. The first three were the inner circle of the "new Israel." But why was Andrew included? In Mark 1:16-20 we have the earliest reference to Jesus calling men to follow him; these four were the first to be called, and now the contents of Jesus' discourse are guaranteed to the church by the authority of these four disciples. They had specifically asked "when" this would be and what would be "the sign when all these things are to be consummated." This inquiry is not two questions, but a single question in a parallel form. Such parallelism was common among Jews, as was also their curiosity concerning a precise time and their inquiry about the sign of the end. The disciples assumed that the fall of Jerusalem and the end of the age were related, even simultaneous happenings.

The apocalyptic elements in the setting are important in Mark's description, but are heightened even more in Matthew. Jesus leaves the temple for the last time, predicting its destruction; the inner circle of the disciples, or "learners", ask the teacher the crucial question concerning the end; and Jesus responds with a prophetic discourse spoken on the mountain "opposite the temple."

Mark 13:5-6, 21-23: *Warnings against false prophets and messiahs*

Jesus did not reply directly, in 13:5, to the question which the disciples had asked in 13:4. In fact, at the end of the discourse their question was regarded as inappropriate (13:32). However, the disciples' concern is not a matter of indifference to Jesus, even though they have asked the wrong question. So rather than a direct answer to a wrong question, Jesus replied with a word of warning: "Take heed that no one leads you astray." The exhortation to take heed is repeated in Matthew 24:4 and Luke 21:8. For Mark, this word of warning is the key idea in Jesus' practical advice, for it is repeated again in verses 9, 23, and 33. The basis for his warning is stated in verse 6—the appearance of pretenders who deceive believers. Verses 21-23 are a part of the same tradition, expanding the idea in verse 6, and concluding with an appropriate warning.

Historically, Israel had been annoyed by false prophets for centuries. Deuteronomy 13:1-5 is a warning against them; the genuine prophets, like Micaiah ben Imlah and Jeremiah, had contended with them (1 Kings 22; Jer. 29). The Zealot movement of the first century A.D. produced a number of pretenders who by means of their signs deceived many (Josephus, *Antiquities*, XX. 5.1; *Wars*, VI. 5.2). Jews sought signs, and these fakers, some of whom were magicians, had demonstrated their powers to the masses.

In sharp contrast, Jesus repeatedly refused to respond to this bait. But this type of religious fanaticism still became a problem in the early church, especially due to the belief in Christ's imminent return. Like unwelcome insects around food at a picnic table, these false prophets and messianic pretenders gathered around the church's anticipated messianic banquet. The warnings, both in 13:6 and 21-22, suggest an immediate danger to Christians. Using his name, the pretenders claimed to be the Christ (Mark 13:6; Matthew 24:23). They authenticated themselves by signs and wonders which deceived believers. The references to "here" and "there" (13:21) suggest a specific place and time. Matthew's reference is even more precise; his statements about their appearing "in the wilderness" and "in the inner rooms" are evidently based on real events (24:26).

Warnings against such fanaticism are found elsewhere in the New Testament. Luke's parallel to Mark 13:5-6 states that those who claim the end is near lead believers astray (21:8). Writing to the Thessalonian church about A.D. 50, Paul tried to deal with a community that had reached a high apocalyptic fever, with some maintaining that the day of the Lord had already come (2 Thess. 2:1-12). The second and third century church fathers, Justin Martyr and Irenaeus, mention individuals who assumed divine prerogatives. In our century, Father Divine and Rev. Moon have been heralded as the Messiah by their followers. Not only their sensationalism, but also their millionaire life-styles, distinguish them from the true Christ, the suffering Son of Man of Mark's Gospel (8:31; 9:31; 10:32-34, 45).

Mark 13:9-13: Warnings about persecution

This paragraph, dealing with the persecutions of the faithful, is bracketed by the structural imperative "take heed" in verse 9 and the call to endurance in verse 13. In content, it consists of three persecution warnings, each introduced by the phrase "deliver up." Matthew 24:9-14 deals with the same subject, although the closest parallel in style is Matthew 10:17-23, which discusses the problems of the young missionary church. Luke also has two versions, a "Logia" fragment in 12:11-12, and a longer account in 21:12-15, which is close to the Markan parallel, though in spirit less pessimistic. Sayings about persecution came to be highly regarded in the early church. The literary variety in the several passages suggests that we are dealing with the same basic subject material that has been developed along several different lines.

There is no doubt that Jesus predicted persecution for himself and his followers. The references to councils and synagogues refer to Jewish tribunals, while kings and governors were Gentile authorities. It is impossible to indicate exactly where these persecutions would occur, although a Palestine locale is likely. We know that Christians first incurred the hostility of Jews, and only later that of the Gentile authorities.

Interestingly, the descriptions of persecution closely fit Paul's experiences as described in 2 Corinthians 11:21-33 and the book of Acts. There may then be a relationship to the Gentile mission referred to in Mark 13:10. This verse does not appear in the parallels in Matthew and Luke. Commentators have questioned whether these words were spoken by Jesus in view of such statements as Matthew 10:5, 23, and 15:24. However, it is difficult to believe that Jesus had a narrower attitude toward Gentiles than Isaiah 40–66, for example. It is thus likely that verse 10 represents the mind of Jesus concerning the Gentile mission, even though it is not his exact words.[8] This mission definitely had an eschatological character in relation to the end of the age.

The suffering of the Christians "for my sake" (13:9, and "for my name's sake"; 13:13) has an ultimate quality of its own.

While they are suffering unjustly, they are not to resist or insist on their rights. When arrested, they should have no anxieties, because the Holy Spirit will give them the words they are to speak. Like the faithful witnesses in Daniel and Revelation, they are exhorted to patient endurance unto the end (Dan. 12:12; Rev. 2:10).

Mark 13:14-20: The sacrilege in the temple

The appearance of the Antichrist in the temple, the flight of believers, the great tribulation, and the shortening of the days for the sake of the elect were elements in the tradition current among first generation Christians. The roots of this belief were in Judaism, beginning with the experience involving Antiochus Epiphanes, and rekindled again in A.D. 40 when the insane Roman emperor Caligula ordered that a statue of himself be set up in the Jerusalem temple. The Jews had bravely resisted this desecration and were on a collision course with him when he was assassinated in January, 41 by one of his own Romans. Memories of these foreign abominations were indelibly stamped on Jewish minds, but they also had a certain shock effect on sensitive Christians.

In spite of the anti-Jerusalem and anti-temple thrust of Mark, a reverence for the temple lingered in his mind. Thus the thought of its coming desolation by pagan Gentile hands evoked a kind of chill that was treated with awesome reserve. This is the mood that characterizes Mark 13:14, where he is urging his readers to think unthinkable thoughts with him. In one of Mark's comparatively rare personal comments, his readers are warned ("let the reader understand") to read with perception. The parallel in Matthew 24:15, by referring directly to Daniel and the holy place, makes explicit what Mark intends to say. His passage is a prophetic oracle based on Daniel (9:27; 11:31; 12:11). Mark is

urging his reader to "see" this prophecy fulfilled in an event soon
to occur. Thus we have an oracle reinterpreted to apply to the
profaning of the temple and the fall of Jerusalem. Luke, writing
to Gentiles after these events had occurred, substitutes the siege
of Jerusalem for the profaning of the temple (21:20).

In urging his readers to "see" the profaning of the temple,
Mark envisions an act performed by a satanically possessed person. While the events of the paragraph are limited to Jerusalem
and Judea, the blasphemy is so horrible that it is portrayed apoc-
alyptically. Drawing on a similar tradition, Paul had warned
Christians that the day of the Lord would not come until the
man of lawlessness, the son of perdition, would come (2 Thess.
2:3-4). Writing some fifteen years later, as the dark war clouds
hung low over Jerusalem, Mark urges his readers to be on the
watch for a final, and ultimate, experience of this abomination.
While the neuter article is used of the "desolating sacrilege",
the masculine participle, "standing" (or "usurping" in NEB),
raises the evil thing to the level of a person. Therefore, the New
English Bible translation of Mark 13:14, "But when you see
the 'abomination of desolation' usurping a place which is not
his," is to be preferred to the RSV or King James translation.
In a view that parallels Paul's warning, the threatening power
has been raised to the level of an evil person. Satan has taken
possession of the temple.

This awful horror sets in motion the events described in the
verses that follow. They remind us of Mattathias' call to the faithful to flee to the hills in the Maccabean crisis (1 Macc. 2:27-28),
though there may also be a basis for the exhortation in Lot's
flight from wicked Sodom (Gen. 19; see Luke 17:28-29). Like
residents in the path of a wall of water from a broken dam, or
families heading for storm shelters before an approaching tor-
nado, believers are urged to flee. Since there is no time to be

lost, forget your possessions and run for your lives! Special concern is voiced for pregnant women and very recent mothers, neither of whom would be in condition for such a flight. An exhortation is made to pray that it might not happen in winter, when torrential rains may fall and no food would be available in the fields (13:18). Matthew, reflecting a Jewish Christian concern, adds "or on a sabbath" in his parallel version (24:20). Reflecting Daniel 12:1, the scene is one of unprecedented tribulation for the believers which will be shortened, however, by God's intervention for the sake of the elect, the faithful remnant (Mark 13:19, 20; Matt. 24:21, 22). Behind these agonizing experiences, God is in control, setting the limits to evil's time and extent. For Luke, the destruction of Jerusalem ushered in the "time of the Gentiles," a period when they would have opportunity to enter the kingdom of God (Luke 21:24).

It is certain that Jesus spoke not only of the destruction of Jerusalem, but also of the profaning of the temple. There is still some question how his words were transmitted, whether by oral tradition or by an earlier written account as the personal comment in Mark 13:14 might suggest. The warning did not fall on deaf ears. According to the church historian Eusebius, when the Roman armies approached Jerusalem, the Christians fled to Pella in Transjordan, where they were safe from the desolation that fell upon the holy city and its temple *(Ecclesiastical History,* III, 5. 3).

Mark 13:7, 8, 24-27: The birth pangs and the parousia of the Son of Man

We reach the climax of the discourse with the parousia of the Son of Man. This section is composed of Old Testament material linked together with apocalyptic ideas of the Son of Man's parousia on the day of the Lord. Two basic presuppositions guided Mark: the Old Testament is inspired Scripture, and Jesus is the Son of Man.

As 13:5-6 is a parallel to 13:21-23, so 13:7-8 is parallel to the cosmic disturbances of 13:24-27. However, the section breaks off at verse 8 with the mention of the birth-pangs. The order of the events in the synoptic Gospels is amazingly close to the woes released by the opening of the six seals in Revelation 6:2–7:1.[9] Wars, international strife, earthquakes, and famines are precursors of the end; but they are only the beginning of the birth-pangs (13:8; Matt. 24:8). From experience, most mothers—and some sensitive fathers—know that these are the most excruciating pains! The apocalyptic birth pangs are cosmic and celestial; the whole creation is in convulsive upheaval (13:24-25; see also Rom. 8:22). In the Old Testament prophecies, from which these sayings are derived, these were symbolic pictures of divine judgments coming upon Babylon and Edom (Isa. 13:10; 34:4). In apocalyptic writings, they become signs of God's direct activity; now he is shaking the heavens as well as the earth (Heb. 12:26-27). And the celestial signs, the darkening of the sun, moon, and stars, are the final woes that immediately precede the fulfillment of God's promises for his people (Joel 2). As the water flows most swiftly just before the falls, so the disturbances are most cataclysmic just before the final redemption. Therefore believers are exhorted not to be alarmed by the events breaking loose around them (13:7).

This cosmic and celestial drama is then the framework for *the* climactic event—the appearance of the Son of Man in the clouds, accompanied by God's angels (13:26-27). Clouds were the vehicles of God's presence in the Old Testament, thus his divine origin is suggested by his coming in this way. The idea comes from Daniel 7:13, where one "like a son of man" comes with the clouds. While the figure in Daniel is likely collective, Mark reinterprets the figure to refer to an individual. Traditional Christians have usually understood "Son of Man" to refer to Christ's humanity, in contrast to "Son of God," which refers to his divinity. Actually, "Son of Man" in the Jewish and early Christian apocalyptic context is the superhuman person who comes from heaven as God's agent to the earth. The references in 1 Enoch 37–71 are prime examples, as are many Synoptic Gospel references. His parousia is the signal for the angels that accompany him to gather the scattered elect ones of God (13:27). The symbol of harvest, which is also apparent in the paragraph that follows, is clearly what Mark had in mind. This is not an occasion for judgment, however, but a redemption event. In the book of Mark, the Son of Man, with the possible exception of 8:38, comes to redeem God's people, though ironically, before the high priest this claim became the ground for convicting him of blasphemy (14:62). Luke omits Mark 13:27 in his parallel account, probably because the Jewish imagery behind it would be difficult for his Gentile readers.

In Mark 13:27 Jesus promised his disciples he would come again. How do we understand and interpret this? Permit me to distinguish between the *fact* and *form* of his parousia. The fact of the promise is Jesus' presence, perceived by faith. The form of his coming varies, with Mark and Matthew accenting the apocalyptic imagery in the drama, Luke lessening it, while John uses even different imagery, that of "light" and "life", to affirm that Jesus is already present with his people.

Mark 13:28-37: The nearness of the parousia

Given the fact of the kingdom's coming, the question concerning *when* it will come remains to be answered. This is the subject of the closing verses of the chapter.

The section begins with a parable and its application (13:28-

29), followed by three short related sayings (13:30-32). The imperatives to "take heed" and "watch", occurring at the beginning and the ending, give structure to the last paragraph (13:33-37). The parable of the doorkeeper summarizes the mood and applies the lesson of the whole section.

The fig tree, which earlier had been the object of judgment (Mark 11:12-14, 20-21), now becomes a symbol of hope. The rising of the sap in its branches and its leafing out were sure signs of the nearness of summer. Originally, at the time the parable was first spoken by Jesus, it probably referred to the time of Jesus' ministry. As summer was the season of gladness in Israel, so his preaching and healing was the season of good news and deliverance, the time of the kingdom of God. This is the application that Luke gave to the parable (21:31). Mark, however, applied the parable to the nearness of Jesus' parousia. Summer suggests the coming harvest with the gathering in of God's people. It is also the summer of gladness, in contrast to the winter of tribulation and woe that will have passed.

The difficult saying in 13:30 has its closest parallel in Mark 9:1 and Matthew 10:23b. Each begins with the words, "Truly, I say to you . . . " and affirms the parousia of the Son of Man (Matt.) or the kingdom of God (Luke) in "this generation." The generation refers to Jesus' contemporaries, and this interpretation is consistent with the lesson from the fig tree parable (see also Matt. 23:26). There can be little doubt that these are authentic sayings of Jesus, especially in view of the preface to each. This admittedly raises difficult questions. The delay of his parousia was a problem in the early church, but believers learned to live with it. When Luke wrote his Gospel, the major problem in the church was no longer the delay of Jesus' parousia, but the failure of Israel to respond to the Gospel.

Since no one, except the Father, knows the exact time of the kingdom's coming, believers must always be on the alert. In contrast to the timetables of Jewish apocalyptic thought, Jesus made no claim to any knowledge of the exact day or hour. Instead he emphasized the unexpected coming of the day of the Lord. It will be a sudden surprise. Paul was echoing this feature of Jesus' teaching when he reminded the Thessalonian believers that the day would come "like a thief in the night" (1 Thess. 5:2; see also Matt. 24:43). In view of this, Jesus told the parable of the doorkeeper to reinforce the command to watchfulness. The disciples are like those servants who were put in charge of the household during the master's absence. This would imply a delay, but the point of the parable is the need to be alert, because the master may suddenly return. The lesson of the parable, with the exhortation *to watch*—"*for* you do not know . . . "—is obvious. Watch! For his parousia is near and yet incalculable. Matthew has put even more emphasis on the theme of watchfulness, expanding the command to be ready in the lessons of the exciting parables of the ten maidens and the talents (Matt. 25).

Conclusion

Jesus gave no direct reply to the disciples' question concerning what would signal the coming of the kingdom because such questioning was inappropriate. Instead, he warned them about the coming suffering and cosmic and heavenly upheavals that would be the birth pangs of the Son of Man's parousia. Since his coming is sure but incalculable, they must always be on the watch, for he will come suddenly.

7 The Book of Revelation

The book of Revelation is a closed book for too many Christians. Equally unfortunate, it has been the happy hunting ground for sectarians who have predicted a timetable of future events. Revelation deserves better treatment than either of these. The symbolic language was not meant to deter, but to inspire its readers. Christians throughout the centuries, especially in troubled times, have received courage and hope from its pages. The opening words immediately give us an important clue concerning how to read the book: "the revelation of Jesus Christ." This phrase states the theme which is the heartbeat of the book: Jesus Christ is revealing himself to his suffering church!

Historical Background

Christianity spread into a world where there was an amazing whirlpool of religions and cults. The province of Asia, in what is now western Turkey, was an interesting example of this mixture of religions in the first century A.D. For centuries, the residents of this rugged and beautiful region, also known as Anatolia, had worshiped their local gods. Every city had its patron deity or chief cult. At Ephesus it was Artemis; its huge temple, which burned on the night Alexander the Great was born, was one of the seven wonders of the ancient world. Thyatira also had a temple to Artemis, as well as a shrine to an Oriental sibyl. At Sardis the chief cult was Cybele, with its eunuch priests leading in the wild worship. In the grape-growing region of Philadelphia, Dionysus was the patron god. Pergamum also worshiped Dionysus as well as Asklepios, who was represented in the form of a snake in the cult worship.

These ancient religions were deeply ingrained in the fabric of Anatolian life. But another religious element was added after the conquests of Alexander. The new colonists brought the Greek gods, which included Zeus, Athena, Hercules, and Apollo, with them, and temples to these deities were eventually built in several Anatolian cities. Then, late in the first century B.C., the earliest visible signs of Roman state religion appeared. In 29 B.C., the Synod of the province of Asia built the first temple to Augustus and Roma, patron goddess of Rome, at Pergamum. Pergamum already had four patron deities; besides the Anatolian deities, Dionysus and Asklepios, temples had been built to the Greek deities, Zeus and Athena. But as the administrative capitol of Asia, Pergamum was also destined to become the seat of the state religion. In the second century A.D., two more temples, one to Trajan and another to Severus, would be built. Modern visitors to Pergamum climb the large, conical hill, 1000 feet high, which is covered with the ruins of ancient heathen temples and altars. Pergamum was a microcosm of Asia. This complex of ancient shrines and temples, whether of Anatolian, Greek, or Roman origin, is solid evidence of the religiosity of the ancient world into which Christianity entered.

The rulers of Rome had practical reasons for promoting the

state religion of the imperial cult. Mighty Rome ruled the world from the damp forests of Britain to the hot sands of North Africa, from the sunny shores of Spain to the exotic Oriental cities of the Middle East. Conquering this vast territory had involved over a century of warfare and bloodshed that finally ended with the "Pax Romana" just a generation before the birth of Jesus Christ. Now the hundred million subjects had to be governed, and this meant developing a loyalty to Rome. Given the centuries of old traditions and customs and the wide variety of people, racially and ethnically, developing a common loyalty or allegiance would not be easy. The practical Roman answer to this problem was emperor worship, and this became the keystone of the Roman imperial policy.

This worship was not entirely new; the honor and worship accorded Alexander the Great and Antiochus Epiphanes were pre-Roman examples. Public enthusiasm for Augustus was behind the building of the temple to him and Roma at Pergamum, even though he laughed at the notion that he was a god. So did the emperors Tiberius and Claudius, but the madman Caligula encouraged it. Even Nero's vigorous persecution of Christians was done for personal reasons; he hated them and used them as a scapegoat to shift blame for the burning of Rome. However, sentiments for emperor worship began gathering force again under Verpasian (A.D. 69-79), who built up the image of his family and himself; though he never declared himself a god, he was called "Benefactor and Savior" by some of his subjects.

His successor, Domitian (A.D. 81-96) capitalized on these sentiments. He was a shrewd and jealous ruler whose prejudices and fears increased with age. Under him, the practice of associating local native religions and and the imperial cult grew. In Laodicea, for example, the festival of Zeus and the festival of Domitian came to be celebrated on the same day. At Ephesus, a large statue of Domitian, three times life-size, was set up in the temple of Artemis. About midway through his reign, he seems to have persuaded himself that he was "God and Lord" *(deus et dominus)* and ordered his courtiers and poets to greet him accordingly. Offerings and libations were made before his statue. Coins were minted with his image on them, proclaiming him "God and Lord." A state religion, with its own shrines and priesthood, was developing throughout the empire. Worship of Domitian was being enforced, and by A.D. 95, Christians were feeling the heavy pressures of this religion. Who is lord—Christ or Caesar? This encounter is the background to the book of Revelation.

The extent of the persecution under Domitian is still a matter of debate. But there is no doubt Christians suffered, and that some even lost their lives. Clement, bishop of Rome at the time of Domitian, refers to "the sudden and repeated misfortunes and calamities which have befallen us" (1 Clement 1:1). At least one Christian, "Antipas my witness, my faithful one," had been killed (Rev. 2:13). He had died at Pergamum, that stronghold of pagan idolatry, "where Satan's throne is," and "where Satan dwells." John, the author of Revelation, was exiled by Domitian in A.D. 95 to the rocky island of Patmos, off the coast of Asia Minor. Though separated from his brethren on the mainland, he shared with them "in Jesus the tribulation and the kingdom and the patient endurance . . . on account of the word of God and the testimony of Jesus" (Rev. 1:9). This is the theme, shaped in the crucible of suffering, for the book of Revelation.[1]

Literary Form and Purpose

An apocalypse, as noted previously, was usually written under an assumed name. The Christian apocalypse is an exception to this. The author identifies himself; "I John, your brother, who share with you in Jesus the tribulation and the kingdom and the patient endurance, was on the island called Patmos on account of the word of God and the testimony of Jesus" (Rev. 1:9). There was no longer any need for pseudonymity, for one greater than the Law had come and had been revealed. Actually, the book is not so much the revelation to John, as it is "the revelation of Jesus Christ" (1:1). We are introduced to the central figure in the very first line; the curtain is pulled back, revealing to the church the drama that must soon take place. Occupying center stage is Jesus Christ. He is the Alpha and the Omega, who is and who was and who is to come. He is the one "like a son of man" whom John sees, resplendent and triumphant, in the midst of the seven golden lampstands. He is thus present among the suffering churches, as the one who died and now lives, holding the keys of death and hades. He is the one who addresses each of the seven churches, and in so doing, the whole catholic church.

John is then the servant who bears witness to this revelation of Jesus Christ by writing to the seven churches. The writing is thus a pastoral work to churches who have endured, and could expect to be called upon to suffer even more persecution. We usually refer to Revelation as a book, though in literary form it is actually a letter. It begins and ends with the literary form of epistles familiar to the churches through the letters of the apostle Paul. Following the title (1:1-3), there is an introductory salutation (1:4-8). "John to the seven churches that are in Asia" was the usual form for beginning a letter. Just as Paul wrote to seven churches, so John is writing to seven churches. The greeting is a benediction from God, just as in the Pauline letters. The final benediction at the close of the book, "The grace of the Lord Jesus be with all the saints. Amen" (22:21) is an unusual ending for an apocalypse, but this is an apocalypse intended to be read in the public worship of the churches. Readers might check for themselves the fact that all the letters of the Pauline corpus, as well as Hebrews, 1 and 2 Peter and Jude end with a benediction, though there is some variety in the exact wording.

The number seven also has great significance for understanding the structure and content. Revelation has seven main sections, generally alternating between a vision of events on earth and those in heaven:

1:1– 3:22:	Introduction and letters to the seven churches
4:1– 8: 1:	The vision of God and of the Lamb
8:2–13:18:	The vision of the church in tribulation
14:1–15: 4:	The vision of the church triumphant
15:5–16:21:	The vision of the seven angels of God's wrath
17:1–20: 3:	The vision of Babylon's overthrow
20:4–22:20:	The vision of the church triumphant

There are seven beatitudes in Revelation,[2] seven spirits before the throne, seven seals, seven trumpets, and seven bowls of wrath. There is profound symbolism in this use of seven, inasmuch as seven suggests completeness and totality. In writing to the seven churches in Asia—though we know there were others there, such as Colossae—John is writing to the whole church. In the sevenfold visions of the seals, trumpets, and bowls he is asserting the totality of God's judgment. The unity of Revelation is an artistic unity, not a chronological or arithmetical unity. "John is like an expert guide in an art gallery, lecturing to students about a vast mural. First, he makes them stand back to absorb a general impression, then he takes them close to study the details."[3] The same basic idea may be expressed in another metaphor. John's artistic unity is like that of a musical theme with variations, each variation adding something new to the significance of the whole composition.

Interpretation of Revelation

The literary form, with its rich symbolism, is used for a pastoral end. The letters to the seven churches in Chapters 2-3 best illustrate this. John is writing to warn and to encourage the churches. There is an urgency in what he writes that mirrors the setting and the vision. "Blessed is he who reads aloud the words of the prophecy, and blessed are those who hear, and who keep what is written therein; for the time is near" (1:3). The so-called "letters" to the seven churches are not letters in the formal literary style of ancient times; they lack both the customary beginning and ending. Rather, they are literary creations designed for the purpose of *warning* (an imperative form of the verb is used) and *encouraging* (a future indicative verb is used) Christians to obedience and faithfulness. They are thus exhortations from beginning to end. Each of the seven "letters" contains promise ("To him who conquers") and warning ("He who has ears to hear, let him hear"). The particular details vary with each church. John, as a good pastor, knows his congregations and counsels them. To the orthodox church at Ephesus which has lost its first love, he writes, "Remember then from what you have fallen and repent." To the poor (yet rich!) and suffering church at Smyrna, he writes, "Be faithful unto death, and I will give you the crown of life." To the church at Pergamum which was compromising with idolatry and immorality, he writes, "Repent then." To the church at Thyatira that was threatened by heretical teachings, he writes, urging them to "hold fast what you have." To the practically lifeless church at Sardis, he writes, "Awake, and strengthen what remains." To the struggling church at Philadelphia, endangered by persecution, he writes, "I am coming soon; hold fast what you have." To the lukewarm church at Laodicea, he writes, "Be zealous and repent."

Interestingly, there is an element of fulfilled prophecy concerning the seven churches. The archaeologist and scholar Sir William Ramsay, who spent years working in the region, has made the following observation:

> Among the seven churches, two only are condemned absolutely and without hope of pardon: Sardis is dead and Laodicea is rejected. These two cities at the present day are absolutely deserted and uninhabited. Two churches only are praised in an unreserved, hearty and loving way: Smyrna and Philadelphia. These two cities have enjoyed and earned the glory of being champions of Christianity through the centuries. Other two churches are treated with mingled praise and blame: Pergamum and Thyatira, both of which still exist as flourishing towns. One church alone was to be removed out of its place: Ephesus, which was moved to a site two miles distant, and is now sunk to an insignificant village.[4]

The scene shifts from earth to heaven with the vision in Chapter 4. The throne of God is central in the vision, which is quite common in apocalypses. A great festival service is about to begin, with the 24 elders, the 4 living creatures, and the 144,000 all participating in the worship.

The 4 living creatures represent all creation, and their "eyes" reveal an intimate knowledge of all God's works (Ezek. 1:5ff.). The 24 elders represent the 12 patriarchs of the Old Testament and the 12 apostles of the New Testament. Both Israel and the church are participating in the heavenly worship. This in turn suggests that the 144,000 represent Israel and the church, God's elect people.

$$\begin{array}{r} 12 \\ \times\ 12 \\ \hline 144 \end{array}$$ Israel's number (tribes)
The church's number (apostles)

$$\begin{array}{r} \times\quad 1000 \\ 144,000 \end{array}$$ A thousand times over

The 144,000 has been understood in a literal and restrictive manner, as though there would be only that number in heaven. The Russellites, now known as the Jehovah's Witnesses, interpreted it that way until their numbers exceeded 144,000. Then they had to find another explanation. John's intention is quite the opposite of this restrictive view. There were probably less than 144,000 Christians in the world when he wrote Revelation. God's election is gracious, expansive, and generous. Their invitation is open; there is yet room.

While the worship is in progress, John sees a scroll in the right hand of him who sits on the throne. The scrolls were letters of investiture with supreme authority. They were legal documents in the ancient world and were always sealed; a legal Roman will, for example, had to be sealed seven times. This scroll is sealed, indicating that what is written on it cannot be altered and is unknown to others. A search begins among the worshipers for one who is worthy to break the seals and open the scroll. No one is found among the worshipers who is worthy, except the Lamb. He is worthy, because he was slain and by his death ransomed men for God and thereby made them "a kingdom and priests to our God" (5:10). Here the nature of the people of God is revealed, and they join with the hosts of heaven in worshiping the Lamb.

The opening of the seals by the Lamb reveals the course of history. The first four seals release horsemen who scourge the earth, and the fifth and sixth seals reveal spiritual suffering and judgment. The empire is seething with those elements that make up the birth pangs of judgment (Mark 13:8). The four horsemen of the apocalypse summarize their tragic story of human vanity, futility, and oppression. The swift succession of conquest, civil war, famine, and death demonstrates what man does when left to his own devices. Yet these horsemen have only a derived authority that is given to them for a time. Their destructive and deadly actions are not the final word in history. But human society is plagued by tragedies until the number of the elect is complete. The souls under the altar cry out "How long?" (Rev. 6:9-11). They are told to be patient and await the end of the persecution. God is a just God who hearkens to the prayers of those who are wronged. A parallel to this conviction is found in 1 Enoch 47:4: "The prayer of the righteous has been heard, and the blood of the righteous required before the Lord of Spirits." The sixth seal reveals cosmic catastrophes which are described in more detail in the later visions of the trumpets and the plagues.

There is a remarkable similarity between the catastrophes released by the opening of the seals in Revelation and the birth-pangs in Mark 13 and its parallels. The order is as follows:

Revelation 6:2–7:1	*Mark 13:7-9, 24-25*
Seal 1: War	1. Wars
Seal 2: International strife	2. International strife
Seal 3: Famine	3. Earthquakes
Seal 4: Pestilence (Death & Hades)	4. Famines
Seal 5: Persecutions	5. Persecutions

Seal 6: Earthquakes, signs in
         sun and moon, stars
         falling, men calling on
         rocks to fall on them,
         shaking of the powers
         of heaven, four destroy-
         ing winds

6. Eclipses of the sun and moon,
   falling of the stars, shaking of
   the powers of heaven.

Matthew 24:6,7,9,29	*Luke 21:9-12, 25-26*
1. Wars	1. Wars
2. International strife	2. International strife
3. Famines	3. Earthquakes
4. Earthquakes	4. Famines
5. Persecutions	5. Pestilence
6. Eclipses of the sun and moon, falling of the stars, shaking of the powers of heaven.	6. Persecutions
	7. Signs in the sun, moon, and stars, men fainting for fear, shaking of the powers of the heaven.

The major difference from the Synoptic birth-pangs is the inclusion of the earthquake with the cosmic signs released by the
opening of the sixth seal. It thus becomes a shaking of the
heavenly powers. The seventh seal is not opened until Revelation
8:1, when it introduces another series of seven, the seven trumpets which bring renewed convulsions in nature.

The drama shifts back to earth in Chapters 8-13, where John
sees the church in tribulation. While the church is on earth she
should not expect to be spared the judgment that falls upon
nature. These convulsions in nature are judgments upon the
wicked; they have a striking resemblance to the plagues of
Egypt. John also views an invasion by a host of horsemen from
the east with the blowing of the fifth and sixth trumpets. The
common belief that Nero would return from the dead and lead

a host of Parthians against the empire probably stands behind this vision. All of these awesome trials were signs of the approaching end time.

The temple is "measured" during the interval between the sixth and seventh trumpets (Rev. 11). The temple is the church, the people of God, not made with hands (Rev. 3:12; cf. also Eph. 2:20 and 1 Peter 2:5). The outer court and the holy city symbolize the church in part of her existence. The angel is ordered to leave the outer court exposed. God does not promise the church security from bodily suffering or death; she is outwardly vulnerable to the full hostility of enemies. When the holy city is trampled underfoot, the faithful will be exposed because they refuse to bear the mark of the beast (13:7, 17). The "trampling of the holy city" is therefore equivalent to martyrdom. The time of this trampling is forty-two months (11:2). This is also the time for the mission of the two witnesses (11:3), the preservation of the woman in the wilderness (12:6, 14), and the time in which the beast is allowed to exercise authority (13:5). It is an evil time; it is the time of great tribulation. It is equivalent to "a time, two times, and half a time" (Dan. 7:25). But as 3½ years, a broken seven, it has its limits. The duration of evil has been limited; evil will have an end.

The two witnesses represent Moses and Elijah. They witness to the divine light of the Law and the prophets; their function is to prophesy and bring repentance. The beast makes war upon them and kills them. Here for the only time there is a connection of the beast with Jerusalem. Allegorically, it is called Sodom and Egypt, because it is heir to their wickedness in crucifying the Lord. Various apocalyptic traditions concerning the transfiguration of Elijah and Moses to heaven are behind the text in Revelation 11:11-12; even Josephus states that Moses was carried to heaven in a cloud (*Ant.* 4.8.48).

The vision of the woman, the child, and the dragon in Chapter 12 sets forth in powerful and vivid language the conflict between the people of God and Satan. This chapter, unlike so much of Revelation that draws upon Old Testament and other Jewish apocalyptic accounts, is not derived from any Jewish source. The woman represents the people of God from whom the Messiah comes. The child who is born to her is taken from the clutches of the dragon to the throne of God. This reminds us of that fascinating passage where Paul writes about dying with Christ and so passing "beyond reach of the elemental spirits of the universe" (Col. 2:20, NEB). The woman flees to the wilderness, where she is safe. The city, coterminous with the empire, was the place of great danger for John. The wilderness is beyond that earthly authority. Now enraged, the dragon goes off to make war on the rest of her offspring, which is the church on earth.

The dragon, who has come from the heavens (12:3-4), has agents in the beast from the sea (13:2) and the beast from the land (13:12). These together make up an evil triumvirate, an "unholy trinity" that persecutes God's people. The beast from the sea, who combines the powers of the four beasts of Daniel, is stirred up by the dragon to persecute the saints. The empire has become Satan's messiah. Authority is "given" to him for a limited period of forty-two months (13:5-10). The beast from the land is the system that enforces emperor worship, exercising the authority of the first beast. This cult had the authority behind it, in the first three centuries of the Christian era, to force people to worship at the emperor's image and it also had the power of Grand Inquisitor. Thus it could brand men with a mark which allowed them to buy or sell; those without this mark were condemned to slow death by starvation.

The beast has "a human number," 666 (13:18). There have been many attempts to interpret this number in order to identify the beast. Mohammed, the Pope, Luther, Napoleon, and Hitler have been suggested through the strange game of gematria. Historically, the number is best explained as the sum of the numerical values of the Hebrew letters that spell "Neron Caesar," which add up to 666. When the second "n" of Neron is dropped, which was an optional spelling, the values add up to 616 and this explains the variant reading of the latter number in several ancient texts. John was not only concerned with a single individual, but to communicate something of the mystery of evil associated with the number. The strange play upon the numbers six and seven is evident in the structure of the book. The seven plagues released at the trumpet blasts are really six plus one; in that extra one, six woes are revealed that are in effect a repetition of the first six. Then there is the seventh in which six vials of wrath are poured out plus one more. At each stage, the seventh number indicates that the plagues and woes and tribulations are in the hand of God. In spite of all the presence and power of evil in the world, it does not have final mastery. In the seventh plague or seventh woe or the seventh vial of wrath, God always intervenes in final judgment.[5] Thus these visions point out the futility of evil in the world; it always falls short and fails. "It was and is not . . . and goes to perdition" (17:11).

With the vision of the church triumphant, the scene shifts abruptly again to heaven (14:1ff.). The redeemed sing a new song before the throne, which is a sharp contrast to the dismal mood of the previous section where the influence of the beast was dominant. Here the 144,000 are the total number of those who have the seal of the Lamb, as over against those who wear the mark of the beast. These visions reassure the church in the midst of her persecution, once again encouraging the saints to endurance (14:12; cf. with 1:9). There is even an appeal to those still on earth to join in the worship of the true God (14:6f.).

The vision of the seven angels of God's wrath (15:5-16:21) is in contrast to the vision of the church in tribulation (8:2-13:18). Now the world is in tribulation. Nature is in rebellion. All that is beastly and awful in creation rises and falls on men in a seven-fold revelation of God's wrath. Revelation 8:7ff. and 16:2ff. have the same order of judgment:

Earth
Sea
Rivers and springs
Sun and heavenly bodies
The citadel of the beast
The river Euphrates
The air

The plagues of Egypt may have served as a partial pattern for describing these disasters, although Stauffer suggests that the horrifying experience of the eruption of Mount Vesuvius in A.D. 79 is the background for these terrible events.[6] The vision presents a picture of unrelieved human suffering that rises in a crescendo. The climax comes when the seventh bowl is poured out; mighty Babylon splits into three parts, the cities of the nations fall, and the cup of God's wrath is drained dry.

John then shifts the reader's attention from the general judgment upon the earth to the particular judgment upon Babylon itself (17:1-20:3). The section opens with a vision of the harlot, who is probably the goddess Roma. She is seated on the beast, dressed in purple and scarlet and bedecked with jewelry. Her splendid appearance demonstrates the pomp and grandeur of imperial Rome. She casts a spell on the whole world with her brilliance, seducing the nations into idolatry or fornication, and making kings and people drunk on the blood of the saints. But this fairy godmother is finally shown in her true light in the judgment, when she is made desolate and naked and ugly. In fact, the beast and the harlot have a falling out and she is ravaged and destroyed by the beast and its ten horns. This is John's vivid way of showing the self-destructive power of evil. He is also preparing the way for the contrast between this wicked harlot and the bride of Christ in all her purity.

And so mighty Babylon falls, and a dirge is announced over the fallen city (18:2-20). The dirge is a scathing economic and political analysis of the Roman empire. Her great wealth is portrayed as the very reason for her fall; the "merchants the world over have grown rich on her bloated wealth" (18:3 NEB). Her self-indulgence and luxury have been accompanied by arrogance and a reckless use of power. This is idolatry in its worship of raw power and mammon. The Christians are called to "come out of her" (18:4), to avoid the entanglements in the evil and punishment of Babylon. Her splendor and wealth and power is only a fleeting and temporary achievement. In "one hour" she is laid waste (18:10, 17, 19); the repetition of this phrase sounds like the strokes of a bell tolling the death knell of proud Babylon. The merchants grieve inconsolably over the city and loss of their wealth. The dirge ends with a call to heaven and the saints to rejoice over her judgment (18:20). Finally, the city's fall is symbolically executed in 18:21-24. In a dramatic act remarkably similar to Jeremiah's (Jer. 51:63-64), the angel throws a stone into the sea, thereby effecting the city's destruction. This puts a stop to all life, commerce, and normal activity in the once bustling city. She is dead! Why? Because of her greed, deceit, and guilt in killing the prophets and saints (18:23). This is a subversive chapter, but so were the early Christians in an idolatrous and evil age! [7]

The theme continues in the judgment of the beast and the false prophet (19:17-21), and the binding of Satan (20:1-3, which is also described in 1 Enoch 54:1-6, 55:4). The evil trinity, so closely allied in persecuting the saints, now shares a similar fate. The cries of the saints under the altar, "How long?" are finally answered in the judgment upon the oppressors and killers of the saints (cf. 18:20 and 19:2 with 6:9-11). Satan is seized and chained, thrown into the abyss for a thousand years. His committal is returning him to his own sphere. He had been cast out of heaven (12:9), now he is cast out of earth, and returned to his own place (cf. 9:11). Then we hear the triumphant "Te Deum" of worship and praise in heaven at the righteous judgment of God (19:1-10).

With the judgment of the oppressors of God's people completed, all is now ready for the vision of the final triumph of God's people. The martyrs are raised to reign with Christ for a thousand years. The thousand years has had a variety of explanations. For the first three centuries of the Christian era, the millenium was usually envisioned as a future period when Christ and his saints would visibly reign on earth for a literal thousand years. This is known as the premillenial view. There were similar Jewish views regarding the Messiah's future reign on earth; 1 Enoch 1-36 and the Testament of the Twelve Patriarchs envisioned a thousand-year future Messianic age. The writer of 2 Esdras believed that he would reign for 400 years (7:28-30), while the Parables of Enoch made no mention of an intervening earthly kingdom of the Messiah between the transformation of heaven and earth.

Origen in the third century and St. Augustine early in the fifth century interpreted the millenium differently, regarding it as the spiritual reign of Christ, rather than a literal thousand years. Augustine maintained that the thousand years represented the period when Christ reigns on earth through the Christian church. For those in whom Christ so rules Satan is bound; the struggle with evil is not over, but Christians know who is Lord and who will finally win. The amillenial view of Augustine recognizes that the imagery of Revelation transcends space and time categories, and thus should not be pressed for a literal fulfillment.

A third viewpoint, no longer widely held, is the postmillenial position. Like amillenialists, holders of this view do not take the thousand years literally, but regard the millenium as the age of the Gospel. However, they view the millenium as the time when not only the church is growing but the world, through Christian influence, is getting better and better. Evil will be overcome, righteousness triumph, and the kingdom of God will come on earth. Then Christ will return *after* the advent of the millenium. Hence, they are called postmillenialists. This view, resting on a naive optimism in human perfectibility, is rejected by traditional Christian churches.

The reign of Christ is interrupted by the loosing of Satan and the final conflict (20:7-10). This latter development is a puzzling interruption of the millenium. Why not throw the key to the pit away and leave Satan there? A theological clue to this dilemma is given in the phrase, "After this he must be loosed a little while" (20:3b). Any logical explanation finally falls short because the loosing of Satan is one element in the wider problem of the mystery of evil. And that mystery is beyond human solution by even the most brilliant human minds!

A clue to understanding and interpreting the final three chapters of Revelation is to read them in relation to Ezekiel 36-48. Israel's salvation, restored to the land, is envisioned (Ezek. 36-37; cf. Rev. 20:4-6). Israel's tranquility is disturbed by the invasion of Gog and Magog (Ezek. 38-39; cf. Rev. 20:7-15). After God destroys the invading forces of wickedness, a new order will emerge with the rebuilding of the temple in the new Jerusalem (Ezek. 40-48; Rev. 21-22).

Death and hades, personified in Revelation 20:11-15, are finally overcome. They are two monsters that have swallowed up all past generations, but now they are forced to yield up their prey in the final judgment. After this massive jail delivery, death and hades are annihilated. They are thrown into the lake of fire, sharing the fate of the beast and his false prophet and of Satan. The insight of the apocalyptist regarding death as the final enemy to be destroyed is similar to that of Paul (see 1 Cor. 15:26, 54).

The end of the old order has finally prepared the way for the vision of a new heaven and new earth. This theme was also promised in the Old Testament and Jewish apocalyptic literature (Isa. 66:22; 1 Enoch 45:4; 72:1; 91:16). The concept of "newness" suggests fresh life rising from the wreckage of the old world. Yet the new Jerusalem is a gift from God. The new Jerusalem comes down from God. In the new Jerusalem God dwells with men. Again, promise is fulfilled in realizing the newness. In Christ, God took up his dwelling and "tabernacled" with men (John 1:14); he indwells his church, which is his temple (Eph. 2:22). Eyes of faith anticipated God's dwelling in the seven cities (Rev. 3:12). God's presence came down to be trampled underfoot by men when God's witnesses prophesied (11:2f.). It has come down like a bride adorned for her husband in the victory celebrations of the Lamb's wedding (19:7-8). Now it comes down to grace the millenium: "Behold the *dwelling* of God is with men" (21:3).

There is a missionary thrust in the closing chapters of Revelation. The suffering of the faithful has been a witness. Where punishment failed to bring people to repentance, the death of the martyrs would succeed. Early in the book, John expressed confidence that the church of Philadelphia would even convert members of the "synagogue of Satan" (3:9). In the closing chapters, this hope is fulfilled in the vision of the "new Jerusalem." *Now* God's dwelling is with his people!

The description of the city in Chapter 21 is patterned on Ezekiel 48:30ff. The city has a wall with twelve gates, representing the twelve tribes of Israel. But there is an important difference in Revelation. Ezekiel had regarded the gates as exits through which the tribes went out to their allotted land; John regards the gates as entrances, open to the nations of the world. As Rome in her time attracted the merchandise of the world (cf. Rev. 18:11ff.), so the new Jerusalem will draw nations into it to worship the living God and the Lamb. He is the source of light and life. The river that flows from his throne is the water of life that waters the city, giving life to trees on either side of the river, and the leaves of the trees are for the healing of the nations.

Conclusion

In the world of many gods and lords, the early Christians worshiped one God, the Father, and one Lord Jesus Christ. In "the Apocalypse of Jesus Christ," he is revealed as the central figure in the drama of redemption. Seven gives not only stylistic unity but also suggests totality in the message of the book. The whole church is addressed; the Lamb of God, worthy through his suffering, is present with his church. Since he has already won the victory, the church, unlike Qumran, does not engage in war but follows the Lamb wherever he goes. The church lives in tension between the present salvation in Christ and the expected future deliverance. This final redemption comes through judgment of the enemies of God. But the end of this judgment is not the triumph of destruction, but the healing of the nations and abundant life together with God in the new Jerusalem.

8 The Vision of Hope

Stability of the times and interest in apocalyptic literature are in inverse ratio. The twentieth century is an age of apocalyptic birth pangs. The arms race and a possible nuclear holocaust threaten all life on our planet. But there are other dangers to it outside the military sphere. The melting of the arctic ice cap, depletion of the earth's ozone layer, theft of plutonium by terrorists, and ill-fated experimentation with weather modification are additional threats. It is not surprising then that there is a steady flow of books that predict the coming doomsday. The secular ones describe the possible disasters, while those of a religious nature view war and cosmic catastrophe as God's judgment on the perversity and apostasy of our age. The very chronology of our century stirs up apocalyptic fever. If we survive Orwell's 1984, we still have to reckon with the year 2000 and its gravitational pull on human imagination and hysteria.

How should Christians respond to this phenomenon? Will the cloud on which Christ comes be an atomic cloud? Should Christian hope be identified with the hysteria that gets publicity in the press and media? I maintain that apocalyptic ideas, viewed in terms of chronologies and time-charts, is a problem, but biblical apocalyptic, understood as a vision of hope, is a possibility for enriching and energizing the faith and life of the people of God.

Apocalyptic as Problem

As stated previously, Jewish apocalyptic ideas were commonly accepted in the early church. Although the figure of a thousand years is mentioned only once in the New Testament (Rev. 20), the idea of a millenial rule of Christ and the saints was widely accepted in the early church. This view, known as chiliasm, was accepted by such prominent church leaders as Irenaeus, Tertullian, and Hippolytus in the second and third centuries. In his later life, Tertullian even joined the Montanist sect. Its founder, Montanus, taught that the New Jerusalem would literally descend to earth in his own province of Phrygia in Asia Minor. (One is reminded of the Moonies who believe that the present-day Messiah will come from Korea!) However, there was also early opposition to chiliasm. The North African theologian, Origen, interpreted the book of Revelation allegorically and understood the millenium in a spiritual rather than in a literal manner.

In the fourth century, Constantine made Christianity the official religion of the empire, and the acculturation of Christianity was in full progress. A change in interpreting Revelation followed, with the church historian Eusebius of Caesarea regarding the age of the church as the beginning of the millenium. St. Augustine refined this idea even more, viewing the thousand years as that age when Christ rules on earth through his visible church. Meanwhile, a debate was in progress whether to accept or reject Revelation as a canonical book. Western Christians generally supported it, while many eastern Christians opposed its inclusion in the New Testament. The important school of Antioch was among the latter, and several early Greek manuscripts did not contain Revelation. But St. Athanasius, the influential bishop of Alexandria, included it among the 27 books of the New Testament in a festal letter in A.D. 367, and this did much to assure its eventual acceptance also in the east. Other Christian apocalyptic books, such as the Apocalypse of Peter and the Shepherd of Hermas, which at one time had enjoyed some support in the early church, failed to pass the test of canonicity and fell by the wayside as authoritative books.

Although the chiliastic enthusiasm waned after Constantine, the idea lingered on like live coals after a fire. As the year 1000 approached, the millenial excitement grew in many parts of Europe due to the belief—a misinterpretation of St. Augustine's view—that a thousand literal years would elapse between Christ's first appearance and his second coming. The English, for example, regarded the fierce Viking invaders under Ethelred the Unready as the incarnation of the Antichrist. In the twelfth century, a Cistercian monk, Joachim of Flora, revived these millenial hopes. In his commentary on Revelation, Joachim maintained that a new age would soon appear. He believed in three successive periods of revelation, each revealing one of the persons of the Trinity. The first was the age of the Father, characterized by the Law and by fear. The second, from the time of Christ up to 1260, was the Gospel age characterized by grace and faith. The third and final age would be that of the Holy Spirit, and would be characterized by love and spirit. Later monks, especially some Franciscans of the thirteenth and fourteenth centuries, regarded themselves as living in this new age with St. Francis as their messianic leader. They rejected the clerical hierarchy, even regarding the pope as the Antichrist, because the third and final age would be a classless society. The revolutionary implications of this were obvious to Thomas Müntzer in the sixteenth century. An early follower of Luther, he became an apocalyptic utopian who wanted to establish the kingdom of God in Münster, Germany. Lutherans clearly rejected this literalism in Article XVII of the Augsburg Confession (1530): "Rejected, too, are certain Jewish opinions which are even now making an appearance and which teach that, before the resurrection of the dead, saints and godly men will possess a worldly kingdom and annihilate all the godless."

Luther and Calvin, while clearly affirming Christ's future return, rejected chiliastic interpretations. However, they contributed little or nothing to our understanding of the book of Revelation. Luther had trouble seeing Christ clearly portrayed in it, and therefore regarded Revelation as a strange and even alien book. John Calvin produced commentaries on every book in the New Testament—except Revelation! Yet both the Lutheran Formula of Concord (1580) and the Presbyterian Westminster Confession (1648) regarded the papacy as the Antichrist.

The English Puritans and the Lutheran Pietists rediscovered Revelation for the Reformation churches. Then, as now, the stresses of the age made apocalyptic ideas interesting beyond the sects and fringe groups. The destruction of the Antichrist and the establishment of the millenial rule of Christ were important themes in Pietism and Puritanism. Philip J. Spener, a German Lutheran pietist, interpreted Revelation in futuristic terms. Another Lutheran, Johann A. Bengel, distinguished two future comings of Christ, the first to destroy the Antichrist and another coming for the Last Judgment. Jonathan Edwards, with his strong Calvinist belief in the sovereignty of God, emphasized the unity of history which would climax in the Last Judgment. However, other Puritans, following the Dutch theologian Coccejus, drew heavily upon the book of Daniel and its successive kingdoms and stressed the divisions of history. Dispensational thought, with its developed schemes and chronologies, emerged from this emphasis. Dispensational writers produce many widely read paperback books today. This is not new, for America has been particularly fertile ground for chiliasts and dispensational ideas. Two examples, although there have been many others, illustrate this. William Miller, basing his calculations on Daniel, predicted that the world would end by fire on October 22, 1844. While thousands of his followers awaited the Lord's coming, the day passed without further incident, but the Seventh Day Adventist movement was born. Charles Taze Russell, again using calculations presumably based on Scripture, predicted that 1914 would be the year of the great judgment; when it did not come, he moved his prediction to 1915. From his preaching came the Russellites, who now call themselves the Jehovah's Witnesses. While they avoid giving a precise date for the final end, they proclaim that "millions living will never die."

This sketchy survey illustrates the recurring problem arising from a wrong understanding of apocalyptic literature. But the chiliasts, with their chronological charts and time schemes, are actually closer to Jewish apocalyptic ideas than to Jesus. The setting of a precise time for the coming of the kingdom of God was common in Jesus' day, but we have noted that he denied such a possibility for humans (Mark 13:32; Matt. 24:36). Most Jews also understood the kingdom in a political and earthly manner; Israel and her Messiah would rule over the nations after a final great war. But Jesus denied the political nature of the kingdom, affirming before Pilate that his kingdom was not of this world (John 18:36). Insofar as they make their own millenial interpretations central, the chiliasts and dispensationalists are living more B.C. than A.D.!

More sophisticated Christians, reacting against chiliastic ideas as well as emphasizing a different world view, have suggested scrapping apocalyptic concepts entirely. In 1900 the influential church historian, Adolf Harnack, stated that apocalyptic was a husk that should be stripped off to get at the real kernel of the Christian message, which he summarized in terms of the immanent kingdom of God and the infinite value of the human soul.[1] Apocalyptic attitudes and literature then become a casualty of human enlightenment and progress, and have interest only as a historical and theological antique. However, the earth-shaking events of the twentieth century have made Harnack's optimism, rather than apocalyptic, antiquated. World wars and the possibility of nuclear holocaust have heated up the ovens from which the doomsday preachers draw their fire. Neither the millenialistic preachers, who have already announced the world's coming obituary, nor the liberal theologians, with their belief in human progress, are biblically on target. The Christian community sails between the Scylla of despair and the Charybdis of human optimism toward its final goal, the kingdom of God. On this journey, apocalyptic is an integral element in eschatology, the doctrine of the last things of the people of God.

Apocalyptic as Possibility

Charles Dickens, in his immortal *A Tale of Two Cities,* referred to the late eighteenth century as the best of times, the worst of times. This paradoxical phrase also appropriately describes our century. Measured by human knowledge and technology, which ease human toil and increase creature comforts, it is the best of times; measured by wars and the possibility for cosmic suicide, it is the worst of times. Despite all the external frills, human nature and experience have not really changed in the last 200, or the last 2000, years. Faith and unbelief, love and hate, hope and despair continue to lift up or burden down the human spirit now as well as in biblical times. We, too, share the dreams as well as the despair of the apocalyptic seers. Given this, we consider the experiences and attitudes of the seers, since it is from their visions that our hopes are finally also derived.

For the apocalyptic seer, God's presence and power was *the* great reality. Like the earlier prophets, he had "seen" the heavenly world where God was enthroned, surrounded by the heavenly host. Enoch, Daniel, John, and other apocalyptic writers testify to this high vision experience; Jesus and Paul must also be included among the visionary seers. They had been given a preview of the divine master plan for earth as it already existed in heaven. The vision itself was an intense, ecstatic event which transcended, even dissolved, space and time as earthly mortals know it. Modern rational man, who like the ancient Sadducee is so apt to deny both angel and resurrection, would be enlightened in the quest for truth by allowing for such a reality and experience. Or to cite the poet Coleridge, he might allow for "that willing suspension of disbelief for the moment, which constitutes poetic faith" (*Biographia Literaria,* Ch. XIV). Yet the seer did not deny the earthly realities, but transmuted and used them to express in pictures the content of the heavenly vision.

Biblical apocalyptic is to be understood then in terms of symbolic realism.[2] The symbols are power and life, not fanciful frills or merely good aesthetics. They are the spark which has kindled, and continues to light fires in human imagination and religious experience, from which in turn art is produced. The Christian apocalypse, for example, has been a prolific source for artistic works—Dürer's woodcuts, selections from Handel's "Messiah," and William Blake's paintings are a few examples. Or consider its power to inspire great Christian hymns. Those with a Scandinavian heritage recall the funeral hymn, "Behold the Host, Arrayed in White." This moving hymn, inspired by the vision recorded in Revelation 7:9, has the power to open heaven to worshipers and give hope in the midst of death itself. In apocalyptic, media and message go together, touching and electrifying intuition and emotion in the deeper levels of the human self.

Through the heavenly vision the seer was given a profound insight also into earthly realities. The charge that religious people are so heavenly minded they are no earthly good does not apply to the biblical seers. Their visions are preoccupied with what is going on or about to happen on earth. Jesus, for example, had a vision of history as a whole in Mark 13; it was a transfiguration of the world, not an escape from it or a denial of it. The focus was obviously not on an interim in a temporal way, though Jesus did see a responsibility and accountability of the nations in the vision of the Last Judgment. Since the seer sees the world *as it should be,* not only *as it is,* he is not a conformist to it. On the contrary, this vision again and again leads him, like the earlier prophets, to break with the temporal powers ruling the world. The vision experience and message is revolutionary. The existing, temporal world is under judgment; in the coming age there will be a startling reversal of existing realities. Thus the seer's vision enabled him to cut through the prevailing earthly idolatries with sharp laser beam precision. Apocalyptic thus strikes a cutting blow against all idolatry.

Idolatry, then as now, takes many forms, but nationalism, materialism, and sensualism are common expressions. Nationalism has been one basic cause for the terrible wars of our blood-drenched twentieth century. In the face of its demands for total commitment, particularly in Naziism and Communism, Christians should recall the "Christ or Caesar" issue which the earliest readers of Revelation faced. In the final judgment, all nations are judged before the righteous God; we recall the vivid scene described by Jesus in Matthew 25:31-46. The seer of a Jewish apocalypse makes this observation:

> Now therefore weigh in a balance our iniquities and those of the inhabitants of the world; and so it will be found which way the turn of the scale will incline. When have the inhabitants of the earth not sinned in thy sight? Or what nation has kept thy commandments so well? Thou mayest indeed find individual men who have kept thy commandments, but nations thou wilt not find (2 Esdras 3:34-36).

Human greed, functioning collectively like soulless leviathans in huge, modern corporations, has moved men to plunder and pillage God's good earth for the almighty dollar. In view of the cultural captivity of many professing Christians to the capitalistic system, we would do well to study Revelation 18 as a commentary of God's judgment on the greedy destroyers of the earth. It is the apocalyptic vision, which pushes the boundaries of God's action back to creation and forward to the redemption of the world, which gives a basis for a theology of ecology. In a society with numerous worshipers at the altars of pleasure and sex, like the Gentile world of the first century, the apostle Paul's words of warning and exhortation go to the very heart of the issue of values and behavior:

> The night is far gone, the day is at hand. Let us then cast off the works of darkness and put on the armor of light; let us conduct ourselves becomingly as in the day, not in reveling and drunkenness, not in debauchery and licentiousness, not in quarreling and jealousy. But put on the Lord Jesus Christ, and make no provision for the flesh, to gratify its desires" (Rom. 13:12-14).

In spirit, this passage is a cousin to the writings of the "sons of light" at Qumran who battled the darkness of their age, but for Paul the solution was not in keeping the Law, but in putting on the Lord Jesus Christ. His apocalyptic message was no cop-out, for putting on Christ meant both the call to watchfulness and incarnating that life of Jesus in the hard realities of the world. When Paul soared into the clouds of apocalyptic imagery (as in 1 Thess. 4:13ff. and 1 Cor. 15:51ff.), he was not acting as a speculative professor, but as a concerned pastor who applied its meaning practically to the faith and life of the believers (see 1 Thess. 4:18 and 1 Cor. 15:58). This inspired apostle lived in both the heavenly heights and the earthly depths, and this gave breadth and stability to his apostolic ministry.

The prophets and the seers were the antennae of the biblical world. While we do not experience their original vision, their vision-message still has power to give insight and wisdom, provided we have eyes to see and ears to hear. "He who has ears to hear, let him hear what the Spirit says to the churches." Physiologists tell us that people with only one eye see all objects on the same plane; consequently, they have no sense of depth. An infant has two eyes, but no sense of depth. As soon as he can grasp objects and walk, he begins to see correctly and move around objects without bumping into them. Christians are so often like infant children who have not superimposed the two images of the world *as it is* and the world *as it should be*. Both perceptions are necessary for the complete picture. The empirical world of sense, without vision, has no depth. But the world as it should be is only an idea until the vision is applied to earthly realities. Christians are called to a stereoscopic vision, with both the eye of sense and the eye of spiritual insight open, and then to superimpose the two in order to see *in depth*. Or to change the metaphor, but express the same idea, we are called to be on the wavelength of the prophets and the seers, the antennae of the world, in order to hear what they are saying to the people of God in this modern age.

The apocalyptic seer, however, saw wider and deeper and higher than even the prophet. Since his vision pushed the horizons back beyond the beginnings of Israel to the creation of the world, he was more interested in Adam than in Abraham or Moses. All mankind became the object of his concern. Enoch was *homo sum*. Jesus envisioned a ministry to the Gentiles, with a final judgment of all nations. Paul appropriately viewed Christ as the Second Adam, whose obedience was greater than Adam's disobedience and whose life therefore would prevail even over Adam's death (see Rom. 5:12-21). In the great chapter on the resurrection, with its several apocalyptic themes, the risen Christ has become the "first fruits of those who have fallen asleep" (1 Cor. 15:20). In other words, Christ's resurrection is the island, emerging out of the sea of death, which is the sign and promise of the whole continent of redeemed humanity that will be raised. Thus the seer's hope is deeper than the prophetic hope, because he envisioned death itself being overcome in the resurrection. So the anchor of hope reaches even to the grave of death itself. This is apocalyptic's greatest message—the tyrant of death is destroyed and Christ reigns in life with his redeemed!

This salvation is cosmic in extent. It is the redemption not only of man but of the creation (Rom. 8:18-23). This passage boggles our finite, temporal minds. But Paul envisions creation too as set free from its current futility and bondage to decay. Its groanings are really the birth-pangs of a new age. There's a new world coming! Paul personifies the creation; it is straining its neck forward, looking eagerly toward the revealing of the sons of God, who have already received the first installment of their redemption with the gift of the Holy Spirit. Hope is faith on tiptoe! Paul's vision is consistent with John's, although the imagery is different. In Revelation, the vision and goal is life with God in the "New Jerusalem" whose final citizenship consists of the ingathering of the redeemed from every nation and all tribes and peoples and tongues. This vision also is cosmic in scope, a new heaven and a new earth where righteousness dwells and life abounds. "Without apocalyptic a theological eschatology remains bogged down in the ethnic history of men or the existential history of the individual." [3]

For the New Testament seers, the people of God live in anticipation. Theirs is a hope that looks both backward and forward. John gives us a glimpse of the worshiping and waiting church in the verse just before the final benediction (Rev. 22:20). The promise of Jesus, "I am coming soon," is placed in the liturgical setting of the eucharist, and the church responds with the prayer —"Come, Lord Jesus." Week after week that prayer was spoken and answered as the risen One made himself known in the breaking of the bread and drinking of the cup. As they gathered "to proclaim the Lord's death until he comes" (1 Cor. 11:26), they remembered the past event of the cross and looked forward to Christ's future parousia. This is the community of the faithful who live with a vision of hope!

Notes

1. What Is Apocalyptic?

1. Hesse, Herman, *Gesammelte Schriften*. IV. "Der Steppenwolf." Zurich: Suhr Kamp Verlag. 1968. Pages 205-206.

2. See Theodore Roszak, *The Making of a Counter-Culture*. Garden City: Doubleday & Co. 1969, for a stimulating presentation of this view.

3. The most widely read book setting forth this position is by Hal Lindsey, *The Late Great Planet Earth*. Grand Rapids: Zondervan. 1970.

4. Russell, D. S., *The Method and Message of Jewish Apocalyptic*. London: SCM Press. 1964. Pp. 37f. The most thorough work in apocalyptic has been done by British scholars. Though somewhat dated, but still unsurpassed in its breadth and depth is the large two volume work by R. H. Charles, *Apocrypha and Pseudepigrapha of the Old Testament*. Volume I: *Apocrypha*. Volume II: *Pseudepigrapha*. Oxford: Clarendon Press, 1913.

2. The Context of Hebrew Apocalyptic

1. See Paul D. Hanson, *The Dawn of Apocalyptic*. Philadelphia: Fortress Press. 1975. This book examines the historical and sociological roots of Jewish apocalyptic eschatology, concluding that the sixth-fifth centuries and second century B.C. were the two most formative periods for the origin of apocalyptic in Israel.

2. This writer finds himself disagreeing with those theologians who maintained that prophecy and apocalyptic had nothing in common. These theologians have generally also claimed that apocalyptic was derived from Persian dualism. Paul Hanson has pointed to the basic methodological error in their approach: "The origins of apocalyptic cannot be explained by a method which juxtaposes seventh and second century compositions and then proceeds to account for the features of the latter by reference to its immediate environment. The apocalyptic literature of the second century and after is the result of a long development reaching back to pre-exilic times, and beyond, and not the new baby of the second century foreign parents." "Jewish Apocalyptic Against Its Near Eastern Environment," *Revue Biblique,* 78 (1971), p. 32.

3. Charles, R. H., *Pseudepigrapha,* Vol. II, p. 421.

3. An Old Testament Apocalypse: The Book of Daniel

1. Rowley, H. H., *Darius the Mede and the Former World Empires in the Book of Daniel.* Cardiff: University of Wales Press Board. 1959.

2. Heaton, Eric. *The Book of Daniel.* London: SCM. 156. p. 209.

4. The First Book of Enoch

1. Charles, R. H., *Pseudepigrapha,* Vol. II, p. 163.

2. Burkitt, F. C., *Jewish and Christian Apocalypses.* London: Oxford University Press. 1913. p. 19.

3. Charles, R. H., *The Book of Enoch.* Introd. by W. O. E. Oesterley. London: S.P.C.K. 1935. pp. xv-xviii.

4. Charles, R. H., *Pseudepigrapha,* Vol. II, p. 238.

5. *Ibid.,* p. 218.

5. An Apocalyptic Sect: The Qumran Community

1. See William S. LaSor, *Bibliography of the Dead Sea Scrolls (1948-1957).* Pasadena: Fuller Theological Seminary Library, 1958, for the most thorough list of earlier articles and information on

the subject. Sensationalist views were propounded, and those views reached a large reading audience, in a work by A. Powell Davies, *The Meaning of the Dead Sea Scrolls,* New York: New American Library, 1956. For more balanced and responsible studies consult books by Millar Burrows, *The Dead Sea Scrolls,* New York: Viking Press, 1955; Frank M. Cross, Jr., *The Ancient Library of Qumran,* New York: Anchor Books, 1961; and William S. LaSor, *The Dead Sea Scrolls and the New Testament,* Grand Rapids: William B. Eerdmans Publishing Company, 1972.

2. See the article by W. H. Brownlee, "John the Baptist in the New Light of Ancient Scrolls," *Interpretation,* Vol. 9 (1955), pp. 71-90. For more detailed scholarly studies of John the Baptist interested readers may consult books by Carl H. Kraeling, *John the Baptist,* New York: Charles Scribner's Sons, 1951; Charles H. H. Scobie, *John the Baptist,* London: SCM Press Ltd., 1964; Walter Wink, *John the Baptist in the Gospel Tradition,* Cambridge: University Press, 1968.

3. See Ethelbert Stauffer, *Jesus and the Wilderness Community at Qumran.* Philadelphia: Fortress Press, 1964.

6. Mark 13: The Little Apocalypse

1. Readers who want a detailed and brilliant survey of the discussion and the issues and persons involved, may consult the book by Albert Schweitzer, *The Quest of the Historical Jesus* (London: A & C Black, 1910; New York: Macmillan, 1960).

2. Bultmann, Rudolf, *The History of the Synoptic Tradition* (New York: Harper & Row, 1963, 1968), pp. 120-130.

3. Beasley-Murray, G. R., *Jesus and the Future* (London: Macmillan & Co., 1954). This book is also the most detailed discussion of the history of interpretation of Mark 13. Colani's interpretation is summarized on pages 9-21.

4. Hartman, Lars, *Prophecy Interpreted* (Lund: C. W. K. Gleerup, 1966), pp. 235-48.

5. Gaston, Lloyd, *No Stone on Another* (Leiden: E. J. Brill, 1970), pp. 41-60. In this learned dissertation, Gaston has also noted that the overall literary form of Mark 13 is that of a "farewell discourse" such as found in John 14–17 and Luke 22:21-38, but the content is different from them because Jesus makes no prediction of his death, p. 42.

6. Avi-Jonah, Michael, Article "Second Temple: From the Roman Conquest until the Destruction." *Encyclopedia Judaica*, Vol. 15. Jerusalem: Keter Publishing House Ltd., 1971, pp. 959-60.

7. Gaston, *op. cit.*, p. 82.

8. Taylor, Vincent, *The Gospel According to St. Mark* (London: MacMillan & Co., 1959), pp. 507-08.

9. See Chapter 7 where this is discussed more fully.

7. The Book of Revelation

1. Revelation continues to receive a variety of interpretations. G. B. Caird, *The Revelation of St. John the Divine* (New York: Harper & Row, 1966) emphasizes the pastoral purpose and nature of John's letter to the first century churches as well as the implications for today. John Wick Bowman, *The First Christian Drama: The Book of Revelation* (Philadelphia: Westminster, 1968), taking a clue from the structure of the book, interprets it as a seven-act drama upon which the letter form has been superimposed. George E. Ladd, *A Commentary on the Revelation of John* (Grand Rapids: Eerdmans, 1972, develops both a historical and futuristic interpretation. In a novel approach, J. Massyngberde Ford, *Revelation* (Garden City: Doubleday & Co., 1975), traces most of Revelation to pre-Christian Jewish sources, with special attention to the disciples of John the Baptist. For emphases upon particular thematic elements from Revelation, readers may consult the works by James Kallas, *Revelation: God and Satan in the Apocalypse* (Minneapolis: Augsburg, 1973); William Stringfellow, *An Ethic for Christians and Other Aliens in a Strange Land* (Waco: Word Books, 1973); Vernard Eller, *The Most Revealing Book of the Bible: Making Sense Out of Revelation* (Grand Rapids: Eerdmans, 1974).

2. In Rev. 1:3; 14:13; 16:15; 19:9; 20:6; 22:7, 14.

3. Caird, p. 106.

4. Ramsey, W. M., *Letters to the Seven Churches of Asia* (London: Hodder & Stoughton, 1904), pp. 432-33.

5. Torrance, T. F., *The Apocalypse Today* (Grand Rapids: Eerdmans, 1959), see pp. 82-90.

6. Stauffer, Ethelbert, *Christ and the Caesars* (London: SCM Press, 1955), pp. 147ff.

7. William Stringfellow, *op. cit.,* develops this chapter in his stimulating and provocative discussion.

8. The Vision of Hope

1. Harnack, Adolf, *What Is Christianity?* London: Williams and Norgate, 1901.
2. Austin Farrer, *A Rebirth of Images: The Making of St. John's Apocalypse* (Boston: Beacon Press, 1949, 1963), pages 19-20, has stated the nature and purpose of symbolic language as follows: "We write in symbol when we wish our words to present, rather than analyse or prove, their subject-matter. . . . Symbol endeavors, as it were, to *be* that of which it speaks. . . . There is a current and exceedingly stupid doctrine that symbol evokes emotion, and exact prose states reality. . . . Nothing could be further from the truth; exact prose abstracts from reality, symbol presents it."
3. Moltmann, Jürgen, *The Theology of Hope* (New York: Harper & Row, 1967), pages 137-138.